Library of
Davidson College

NAZI WAR CRIMINALS IN AMERICA:
Facts...Action

THE BASIC HANDBOOK

By Charles R. Allen, Jr.

ISBN 0-934215-00-6

364.13
A425In

Published by Highgate House
New York, New York 10040-9998

Copyright © 1985 by Charles R. Allen, Jr.

Library of Congress Cataloging in
Publication Data
Allen, Charles R. Jr.
   Nazi War Criminals in America:
   Facts... Action
   The Basic Handbook
   Bibliography: pp. 14
   Includes Index.

89- 9715

1. War Criminals, Nazi in United States
2. U.S. Government and Intelligence, and Nazi War Criminals, Utilization of
3. Cold War Policies and Utilization of Nazi War Criminals
4. Post-Holocaust, Jewish and Other Nazi Genocides, Implications of (1944-1985)

(Parts of *The Basic Handbook* appeared in *Nazi War Criminals in America: Facts... Action*, co-authored by Charles R. Allen, Jr. and Rochelle Saidel-Wolk. Copyright © 1981 by Charles R. Allen, Jr. Productions Inc. *The Basic Handbook* is a new, far more comprehensive and larger work that directly reflects its burgeoning subject.)

In Memoriam: Julius Schreiber, survivor of Auschwitz, whose life ennobled the hopes, dreams and struggles for a world free of racism, bigotry, fascism and war. Dedicated further to Diane, Derek, Jacob and Benedict — the generation young, compassionate and powerful, charged by the legacy of Julius Schreiber to do justice...

Contents

	Page
The Basic Questions: Who, How, When, What, Where...	1
Who Are They?	8
Denaturalization Cases	
Deportation Cases	
Cases "No Longer Active"	
Predicted Prosecutions	
Did You Know That?	29
The Lithuanian 2nd Battalion	32
Furor Over America's Use of Nazi War Criminals	33
• Robert Jan (Jean) Verbelen	
• Klaus Barbie, U.S. Intelligence and the Catholic Church	
• The LaVista Report and the Vatican-Nazi Connection	
• The Arrow/Cross Fascist, Ferenc Vajta	
• Some of the Illegals, 1945-1950s	
Nazi Rocket Scientists, Men on the Moon — And the CIA	49
• The Case of Dr. Arthur L.H. Rudolph	
• Former CIA Chief Defends Use of Nazi War Criminals	
• Other Paperclip Nazis:	
• Dr. Georg Rickhey, Rudolph's Boss at Dora	
• Dr. Krafft A.F. Ehricke and Lyndon LaRouche	
• Dr. Werner Frhr. von Braun, NSDAP, SS	
Deportation: When?...How Many?...To Where?	58
OSI's Trials: Claims vs. Actuality	64
• Charting Denaturalization Cases	
• Charting Deportation Cases	
• Charting Cases "No Longer Active"	
• Summaries and Some Salient Aspects	
The Mengele Case: U.S. Involvement?	70
Right Wing Drive Against OSI	84
Unfinished Business	85

	Page
What Background Material Is Available?	86

- Books, Booklets, Anthologies, Monographs, Papers, Theses
- Major Magazine and Newspaper Articles
- Newspapers
- Television
- Radio
- Anglo-Jewish Newspapers
- Anglo-Jewish Magazines
- U.S. Government Hearings/Publications

Action: What Can You Do?
- U.S. Government Officials — 98
- National Organizations
- International Organizations
- Local Organizations

Critical Comment on Nazi War Criminals: Facts...Action	101
Index	105

About the Type... A Note to the Reader

Some publishers take the time to tell the reader what kind and style of type was used in printing a book. A few even give a brief history of the type.

All too often, however, such remarks are written so as to intimidate the reader somewhat with technical jargon and a stiff-necked, condescending tone. Most such notes are tagged on at the end of a book.

We feel that you might appreciate such interesting information up front, almost precisely at the place you start your read. After all, the book is yours. You are investing valuable time, effort (not to mention your money) in it. Without you, indeed, there would not have been much purpose in putting it out.

We have selected the type with a view toward making your read not only easy and clear on the eye but also pleasant along with a bit of variety in the type you usually see.

This book is made of Times Modern which was designed by a team of graphic artists at AM Varityper in East Hanover, New Jersey. Its primary creator was John Lamprakos whose goal was to fashion not merely an improved type but one that would prove effectively applicable to and advance the state of the art in today's world of printing: computerized electronic typesetting and offset production.

Times Modern derives from the venerable Times Roman, a popular choice in newspapers and magazines ever since its creation in 1932 by the English typographer, Stanley Morrison of *The Times* of London.

Times Modern, however, is distinctively a recent, creative response to the swift advances of technology since the Letter Press. (And in saying such, we do not mean to make invidious comparisons. By no means.)

Moreover, Times Modern is not merely a refinement but a distinctive letter in and of itself, according to its creators.

Barbara Davis of Michael William Printery in Cohoes, New York, who directed the printing and production of this book, considered the virtues of Times Modern as follows:

"The type has a slightly heavier, more durable weight and a body with stronger serifs. (A serif is that part of a letter which juts out from its main body.) Times Modern also possesses a slight condensation, a tighter and more precise spacing that gives a greater character count to a line. In sum, Times Modern provides efficiency and an economy of space while assuring a high degree of readability."

We hope you agree and find Times Modern delivers a clear, pleasurable addition to your own art — that of reading....

A Further Note:

What **The Basic Handbook** Is About, And Where Its Author Is Coming From...

The Basic Handbook is just that: a book that you can have at hand for quick, easy and accurate reference about Nazi war criminals who have been living freely among us since the end of World War II.

Its subject has only relatively recently captured the attention of significant numbers of Americans. Until the late 1970's, it was known to but a few, and even fewer were exercised by the facts of their presence.

With this most welcome increase in awareness, however, there inevitably has come a great deal of tawdry exploitation along with massive distortion and falsehood. The motivation behind such exploitations has of course been the acquisition of quick money, lots of it.

But the subject matter is too vast, complicated and subtle for shallow commercialization. One is required to be scrupulous with facts, respectful of documents and, especially with the eyewitness testimony, exceedingly careful in approaching what is a delicate history: the better to communicate, the better to understand it.

The Basic Handbook tries to give you concisely the essential information you will need to answer such basic questions as: Who are they? When did they get here? How did they get in? How many of them have come here? Where do they live? What have they been doing since becoming citizens or residents of America? Have any ever been used by the U.S. government? If so, how many? What is the proof?

The Basic Handbook further offers the developed facts about U.S. government utilization of charged Nazi war criminals.

Some of the cases so highlighted on the pages that follow may already be familiar to you: Klaus Barbie, Josef Mengele, Archbishop Valerian Trifa. They have been headline news for some time.

Others are hardly household names: Artukovic, Hilger, Laipenieks, Rickhey, Rudolph, Strughold, etc. et al. Yet these figures are of even more importance, more significance because they are today directly our own responsibility. And *Nazi War Criminals in America* is our central concern.

They and those American officials and agencies of government who aided and abetted them, who used them are here among us. And something can be done about them, well beyond what has already been accomplished to date.

That is why *The Basic Handbook* has an *Action* section so that those who are moved to act may have the information needed to do so.

The Basic Handbook also provides the fundamental facts concerning the world-wide controversy which my writings were able to generate on the so-called LaVista Report of 1947. That hitherto "Top Secret" investigation carried out by the U.S. State Department — a report whose historicity can not for a moment be questioned — detailed the workings of the "monastery routes" over which some of the most notorious Nazi mass murderers escaped from post-Holocaust Europe with the knowing assistance of certain prelates of the Roman Catholic Church.

In the section titled "The LaVista Report and the Vatican-Nazi Connection," there is the essential information of American intelligence involvement in this controversial and delicate question.

Just how much — if anything — did Pius XII and the Vatican hierarchy know about these "illegal emigration" routes and their employment by Nazi war criminals and collaborators?

The Basic Handbook also contains vital materials that you can not find anywhere else, nor in such condensed form. All of the 45 trials which the U.S. Justice Department's Office of Special Investigations (OSI) has conducted to date against charged Nazi war criminals are categorized and analyzed here. The scope and depth of these analyses go far beyond anything issued by the OSI or U.S. Congress.

The consequent analyses raise questions that will not provide comfort to those who may have become complacent about *Nazi War Criminals in America.*

Also keep in mind that *The Basic Handbook* has been purposely written and designed to serve as an introduction to the two larger volumes which will follow: Vol. I, *From Hitler to Uncle Sam: How American Intelligence Used Nazi War Criminals* and Vol. II, *A Nation Indicted: America's Nazi War Criminals.*

I trust that *The Basic Handbook* will be as useful as its earlier antecedent, about which Ralph Blumenthal, the Nazi war criminal expert of *The New York Times,* said: "It is excellent for beginners and very helpful for the already initiated." So no matter what level of expertise you may bring to the subject, perhaps *The Basic Handbook* will enhance your own understanding.

Please do not hesitate to get in touch with me with any comments, criticisms or suggestions you may have. I would welcome your thoughts.... Now, let's get on with the read.

Charles R. Allen, Jr.

Who Are They?

Immediately after World War II, an undetermined number of individuals implicated in Nazi genocides, persecutions and other war crimes made their way to the United States.

Where Did They Come From?

Most of the accused Nazi war criminals and collaborators came from Eastern Europe and the Soviet Union. Many are still wanted there for war crimes and treason. Few are of German origin. Most of the crimes of the Holocaust were committed in Eastern Europe and on the soil of the Soviet Union by Nazi Germany and its collaborators.

How Many War Criminals Are Here?

Estimates vary. The Office of Special Investigations (OSI) of the U.S. Justice Department is charged with investigating and prosecuting for denaturalization/deportation alleged Nazi war criminals residing here. Its former director told Charles R. Allen, Jr. that he worked "from a file of some 470" cases. The OSI estimates that "somewhat more than a third" of its own official list have died. Allen has compiled his own detailed list of 323 individuals against whom substantial war crimes charges have been made. Some 36 percent of the accused on his list are deceased.

Other claims that "more than 3,000 war criminals" have found haven in the U.S. have not been proven. However, it is reasonable to assume that during the nearly four decades since the end of World War II, at least 1,000 have come here freely under U.S. immigration laws, especially the 1948 Displaced Persons Act (DPA).

Former OSI director, Allan A. Ryan, Jr., asserts flatly after his retirement from government, that "10,000 Nazi war criminals entered the U.S. after the war." Mr. Ryan concedes that his "estimates" are "hardly scientific." In fact, they are conjecture.

As early as 1949, the German-language newspaper *Aufbau* in New York published a listing of 38 individuals that originated with a survivor named Simon Wiesenthal, later the world-famed Nazi hunter. (That list was incomplete, often used last names only, was filled with misspellings and was otherwise imprecise, and, in fact, inaccurate.)

In 1963, *Nazi War Criminals Among Us* (by Charles R. Allen, Jr.) was the first work to seek out and document charges against sixteen accused

Nazi war criminals and collaborators. Evidence obtained by Allen after 1963 suggested that possibly 22 more might have been in the United States at that time. Thus by the mid-1960's, the unofficial estimate was 38. In the late 1960's, the World Jewish Congress had compiled its listing of 59 such individuals, many derived from Allen's published findings.

Thus from the first reports of 1949 through to the carefully checked and computerized listings of the 1980's, the incontestable fact remains: scores, if not hundreds, of Hitlerian genocidists and collaborators made safe passage to the United States. Exactly how many may never be known. According to an Israeli intelligence report of 1961, the United States was the third largest refuge for Nazi war criminals in the world — after West Germany and Argentina.

Where Do They Live?

No area is "immune" to their presence. Vilis Hazners, an accused Latvian war criminal, lives in a hamlet in upstate New York. Large cities such as New York, Philadelphia, Baltimore, Chicago, Cleveland and Los Angeles have ongoing trials. Valerian Trifa, a denaturalized Romanian Orthodox archbishop deported in 1984, lived in a fortress-like villa in Grass Lake, Michigan. There are proceedings in Florida and Connecticut. Other alleged Nazi war criminals, not yet prosecuted, live throughout the country. Some are or have been employed at prestigious universities, colleges and corporations.

What Are They Accused Of?

They are accused of various crimes ranging from individual to mass murders, from acts of persecution to high-level responsibility for institutionalizing concentration and death camps; from carrying out experiments on humans to top-level implementation of the Nazi genocide program between 1939 and 1945. Most of those on the OSI lists were low-level operators: concentration and death camp guards and guard supervisors, members of execution and punitive squads in collaborator armies, Gestapo agents and informers. Some, however, were complicit at much higher levels: as diplomats, in the secret police, the military, the SS *(Schutzstaffel)*. Many were leaders of the treasonous Fifth Columns of their native lands — the Iron Guard or Green Shirts in Romania, the Arrow/Cross in Hungary, the Iron Wolf in Lithuania, the Thunder Cross in Latvia, the Black Shirts in Italy, the Ustashi in Yugoslavia and the like.

Who Made These Charges?

War crimes documentation centers, ministries of justice, concentration camp survivors and resistance groups from: Poland, Romania, Hungary, Bulgaria, Yugoslavia, Czechoslovakia, the German Democratic Republic and the Soviet Union; Holland, Belgium, France, the Federal Republic of Germany, Denmark, Italy — and Israel.

When Were The Charges First Made?

As early as 1948. Yugoslavia formally requested in 1951 the extradition of one Andrija Artukovic, the Minister of Interior of Nazi-occupied Croatia. He is accused of direct responsibility for the genocide of some 600,000 Serbians, Croations, Gypsies and some 78,000 Jews. The U.S. Justice Department is still seeking his deportation. Substantiated accusations were published by several journalists, including Drew Pearson, Walter Winchell, Milton Friedman of the *Jewish Telegraphic Agency* (JTA), as well as several U.S. Congressmen in the late 1950's and 1960's. Concern over Nazi murderers was stirred briefly in the mid-1960's by Charles R. Allen, Jr's., *Nazi War Criminals Among Us*. Subject resurfaced in the mid-1970's. It has since become a national issue, as yet unresolved.

Did The United States Government Know?

Yes, from the beginning. Several government agencies — the State Department, the intelligence branches of the Army, Navy and Air Force, as well as the CIA, FBI, Radio Free Europe, Radio Liberty and others — knowingly (and covertly) brought some of them into the country. They were used as "contract agents" and "consultants." From 1948 to the late 1970's, these government agencies flatly denied their utilization of war criminals.

What Has Congress Done About Them?

In the mid-1970's, Rep. Joshua Eilberg (D-Pa) and Rep. Elizabeth Holtzman (D-NY) of the U.S. House of Representatives Judiciary Committee succeeded in putting the issue on the Congressional agenda. (At about the same time, a former concentration camp guard supervisor, Hermine Braunsteiner Ryan, was extradited to West Germany for trial;

Immigration and Naturalization Service (INS) attorney Vincent Schiano and investigator Anthony DeVito left the INS, accusing that agency of years of cover-ups on the Nazi war criminal issue.)

Prodded by Congressional forces, INS set up a Special Litigation Unit (SLU) in 1977, headed by Martin Mendelsohn. By 1979, there was widespread dissatisfaction with both the INS and its SLU. Rep. Holtzman, by then Chairperson of the Judiciary Subcommittee on Immigration, used her clout to transfer SLU to the Criminal Division of the Justice Department. It became the Office of Special Investigations (OSI) in 1979.

In January 1977, Congress requested an investigation to determine whether U.S. government agencies had obstructed investigations and prosecutions of alleged Nazi war criminals. On May 15, 1978, the General Accounting Office (GAO), the investigative arm of the U.S. House of Representatives, issued a report. GAO found no evidence of a "widespread conspiracy" within the government to cover up the Nazi war criminal cases, but the FBI and CIA did admit officially for the first time that they had "utilized" Nazi war criminals and collaborators. On July 19-21, 1978, the House Subcommittee on Immigration held hearings on the GAO findings.

On February 6, 1981, Rep. Hamilton Fish (R-NY) and Rep. William Lehman (D-Fla) were joined by over 100 members of the House in signing a letter to President Ronald Reagan, urging the President to give the OSI his full public endorsement. In April 1981, Sen. Christopher Dodd (D-Conn) and 11 other Senators sent a letter to President Reagan, urging him not to cut the OSI's budget for the 1982 fiscal year. The Senators also recommended that Attorney General William French Smith "take a personal interest" in the OSI.

In the mid-1980's, OSI's budget has been kept at about $3.3 million. In 1982, the House Judiciary directed GAO to probe further into U.S. intelligence use of Nazi criminals. By 1985, no GAO report was issued; no hearings had been held; mid-1985 seen as earliest for report's release.

Who Is Prosecuting Them?

Beginning in 1973, a series of task forces and prosecution units were set up first in the INS and then in the Criminal Division of the U.S. Justice Department. In 1979 the OSI was launched with a budget of $2.3 million. Former Nuremberg prosecutor Walter Rockler was OSI's first director. On April 1, 1980, deputy director Allan A. Ryan, Jr. succeeded Rockler. Ryan took leave in March 1983 to investigate U.S. government utilization of Nazi war criminal Klaus Barbie, who was expelled from Bolivia to France. Deputy director Neal Sher was appointed OSI director on November 29, 1983. The present staff of 47 includes 18 lawyers, four investigators and six historians. Denaturalization cases are tried in U.S. district courts; deportation hearings are argued before U.S. Immigration and Naturalization Service administrative courts. A $3.275 million budget was appropriated for OSI for Fiscal Year 1985.

How Many Cases Are There?

In January 1980, the OSI files contained the names of 413 individuals charged with Nazi pasts. By January 1981, there were 233 "active" cases. By February 1981, the OSI had reviewed for triability and closed a total of 231 cases. Thus 180 cases were examined in 1981 for triability, according to the OSI. By late 1984 there were 28 cases in various stages of litigation. Of these cases, defendants are accused — in descending numerical order — of atrocities in the Ukraine, Latvia, Lithuania, Byelorussia and Estonia. The only two of any prominence were Archbishop Valerian Trifa, Romanian Iron Guardist, and Andrija Artukovic, Croatian Minister of the Interior under the Nazis.

A 1984 Congressional Report (No. 98-759, U.S. House of Representatives) gave a total figure of 382 cases of which 182 have been closed out since 1979. The report stated that in 1984 the OSI received 80 new allegations, that 274 investigations "remained pending," and 35 cases were in the courts. The report noted that the OSI "had inherited" 350 cases from the 1972-78 records of the SLU and Nazi War Criminal Task Force of the INS; of these, it recorded that 276 have been closed. (It was not clear whether the 182 cases reportedly closed by the OSI since 1979 included the 276 INS cases mentioned here.)

The OSI was also quoted in the report as having claimed that "approximately half a dozen cases . . . were developed completely [by OSI] *not* from outside sources." These new efforts are scheduled to go to court over 1984-85.

In brief, the Government originally had about 500 case files in 1972. By 1982, the number had dwindled to 325. By end 1984, OSI was working on 201 "live" cases. Virtually all of the basic 500 cases derived from outside — many private — sources, *not* the U.S. Government.

How Did They Get Here?

Many Nazi war criminals came here under the first Displaced Persons Act of 1948-50, entering as legitimate DPs. In some cases, they were secretly requested by various agencies of our government, including the State Department, CIA, FBI, Voice of America, Radio Free Europe and Radio Liberty. They were used for various Cold War activities. According to FBI Report (WFO 65-10649), Nov. 15, 1967, "a total of 1,558 foreign scientists" — 97% of whom were "German and Austrian scientists," the FBI learned — were brought to the United States through a Pentagon-State Department-Intelligence operation called Project Paperclip. Most were minimally members of the Nazi Party; some were SS, and war criminals. (Figures regarding the total number of Paperclip specialists employed by the United States differ. Clarence Lasby's *Project Paperclip,* 1975, states that 642 Paperclippers entered between May 1945 and December 1952. *The Bulletin of Atomic Scientists*, April 1985, asserts without supporting documentation that 765 came in between 1945 and 1955.)

Of OSI's 28 pending cases, 23 are implicated in utilization by the U.S. Government.* At least 156 alleged Nazi war criminals have been utilized by the U.S. intelligence agencies over the past 39 years, research by Charles R. Allen Jr. suggests. Of these 156, most were used *after* their arrival in the U.S. Not a single war criminal or collaborator, moreover, was barred at his or her American port-of-entry because of war crimes or collaboration. Entry was established in Europe via "clearance" processes.

*(The 1981 booklet incorrectly stated that seven of the then twenty ongoing cases were so involved. The number should have been *seventeen*.)

When Did They Come Here?

Most arrived in the late 1940's and early 1950's. The earliest arrival among OSI's pending cases is Bronius Kaminskas (May 1947). Artukovic arrived as a "temporary visitor for pleasure" in July 1948; three years later deportation proceedings against him were initiated. The latest entry date among OSI's list of trials is Anatoly Hrusitzky's, September 3, 1959. Edgars Laipenieks, a CIA agent, entered the U.S. for alien residency in 1960, but was reportedly in the country as a "tourist" on several occasions as early as 1947.

How Long Do Their Trials Take?

According to former OSI director Ryan, "If we file an airtight case against a naturalized American citizen tomorrow and there are no judicial delays, it would still take eight years to complete a case" (*JTA Daily News Bulletin,* June 3, 1980). Deportation proceedings against Artukovic have been outstanding since 1951. After more than 30 years of massive indifference, proven cover-ups and sheer ineptitude, no case is "airtight." Begun on August 15, 1977, the denaturalization case of Feodor Fedorenko was decided in favor of the Government by the U.S. Supreme Court on January 21, 1981. Fedorenko's was the first Nazi war criminal case to be completed at this highest level. Deportation proceedings commenced March 5, 1981, completed December 1984. His case consumed more than seven years. Under the present system, defendants can (and do) stretch their cases well past seven years. Some legal experts argue that this process may be considerably shortened, while still maintaining full due process.

Admitting Waffen SS and Fascist Collaborators...

Mr. Tripp: "We did...stop some people whom we found out through our [Immigration and Naturalization Service] examination, not through the Berlin Document Center [State Department's records] had been members of a German military unit... they had participated in a movement hostile to the United States. We had a very good case, a Latvian who took considerable pride in the fact that he not only had been accepted in their [Germany's] Waffen SS but he had...acquired the status of a commissioned officer. On appeal to the INS Board of Immigration Appeals, that man was ordered admitted, and thereafter most of those who served in the [Nazi] military service...would be admitted...."

Mr. Eilberg: "During what period of time was that?"

Mr. Tripp: "...oh, late spring 1949...That [admission policy] included not only the Waffen SS but...other Units, the Ukraine Brigades [Galician Waffen SS], Vlasov's Army, Hlinka [Czech] Brigade...Unless we had other information [about specific persecution]...apparently it was a Congressional desire that they [Nazi unit members and collaborators] not be kept out because the 1950 amendment to the (1948) Displaced Persons Act...did not specifically direct that they be excluded."

Mr. Almanza Tripp, Former INS Official
Charged in Europe with Administering DPAct, 1948-1950

U.S. Congressional Hearings — July 20, 1978
(Part 2, Serial #39, "Alleged Nazi War Criminals," p. 102)

Who Are They?

(Status of cases as of late April 1985. Subject to change. Information based on OSI Digest of Cases in Litigation. Listed alphabetically, last name first.)

Denaturalization Cases

Artishenko, Basil — accused by OSI of having participated in "execution and persecution of about 100 unarmed Gypies...women and children" as member of, police force in Byelorussia during World War II. OSI filed complaint November 12, 1982. Depositions of Soviet witnesses taken June 1983. Trial scheduled for winter 1984 was postponed. No trial date set as of November 1984. Resides East Brunswick, N.J. Born Byelorussia, 1923. (See *Cases No Longer Active.*)

Gudauskas, Vytautus — case filed June 4, 1984. Served in Lithuanian Police 2nd Battalion, *(Schutzmannschaft)* active in persecution and murder of Jews in Kaunus, Lithuania and Byelorussia, 1941-1943. Resides Worcester, Mass. Born Lithuania, 1918.

Hrusitzky, Anatoly — Ukrainian police officer charged by OSI on August 9, 1983 with having concealed his participation in "persecution and murder of unarmed Jewish men, women and children living in Cherny Ostrov" region of Ukraine. OSI videotaped interviews/depositions of eyewitness survivors in Ukraine. Defendant admitted October 31, 1983, he had served in Ukrainian police unit. Naturalized June 20, 1975, New York. Resided Fla. Born Ukraine, 1917. (See *Cases No Longer Active.*)

Juodis, Jurgis — charged with "assault, arrest, detention and murder of unarmed Jews and others" while officer in Lithuanian Police Battalion (*Schutzmannschaft*) operating in Lithuania and Byelorussia between 1941-1944. OSI complaint filed October 26, 1981. No trial date set, early 1985. Resides Fla. Born Lithuania, 1911.

Kairys, Liudas — accused by OSI on August 13, 1980, of serving with various SS commando guard units (*Wachmannschaft*) in Poland, including Treblinka. Court appointed counsel to represent defendant. Trial began June 14, 1982. Accused of "persecuting unarmed Jewish civilians" at death camp Treblinka. Trial ended July 7, 1982. No decision as of November 1984. Resides Chicago, Ill. Born Lithuania, 1920.

Katin, Matthew — case filed November 1984. Accused of serving in Lithuanian *Schutzmannschaft*. Resides Norwood, Mass. Born 1914.

Klimavicius, Jonas aka, Klimaitis, Jonas — case filed May 30, 1984. Served in 2nd Lithuanian Police Battalion, (*Schutzmannschaft*) active in persecution and murder of 3,800 Jews, Communists and others in Kaunas and Byelorussia. Member of terrorist Iron Wolf. 1941 Gestapo reports list him working with *Einsatzgruppen* squads, 1941-42. Resides Portland, Me. Born Lithuania, 1907. (See *Predicted Prosecutions — Who Are They?*)

Kowalchuk, Sergei and Mykola — brothers accused of atrocities while members of Nazi-controlled Ukrainian police in Luboml, Poland. Sergei was charged by OSI on January 13, 1977 with having "participated, 1941-1942, in the persecution...and commission of crimes against Jewish civilians" while a member of the Nazi collaborating police in Luboml, Ukraine. On July 1, 1983, court ordered Kowalchuk stripped of his citizenship. Appeal process began on August 3, 1983. On September 11, 1984, Fifth Circuit Appeals reversed. Appeals Court ruled that OSI did not prove defendant's "voluntary" enlistment as Nazi collaborator. Ruling was 2-1. Majority also indicated distrust of Soviet videotaped eyewitness testimony. On OSI petition, Appeals Court in late fall 1984 agreed to review decision *en banc* (i.e., with the full Appeals panel of 11 judges). Born Poland, March 15, 1920. Resident of Philadelphia, Pa. Citing death of key witness, OSI moved to dismiss complaint against Mykola, June 5, 1981. (See *Cases No Longer Active.*)

Kungys, Juozas — charged with participation in mass murders of Jews and other peoples as collaborator in Lithuania, "in association with the armed forces of Nazi Germany." OSI complaint filed September 22, 1981. Court ruled for defendant, September 28, 1983, stating government did not sustain burden of proof. U.S. District Judge H. Curtis Meanor accused OSI of "trying to ram through" the case. OSI has appealed ruling. Decision awaited since May 4, 1984. Resides in largely Jewish neighborhood in Clifton, N.J., age 68, Lithuanian-born.

Palciauskas, Kazys *,** — charged with having concealed serving Nazis as mayor of Kaunas, Lithuania, 1941-1943, assisting in persecuting civilians, ordering internment of Jewish population of more than 20,000 in ghetto, confiscating Jewish property, forcing Jews to wear yellow stars, and signing deportation orders. OSI complaint filed June 15, 1981. Trial commenced December 6, 1982; concluded December 10, 1982. Judgment in favor of OSI, March 23, 1983. On appeal, Eleventh Circuit Court fully affirmed lower court's decision. Awaiting action toward deportation hearing as of November 1984. Resides Fla. Born Lithuania, 1907. (See *Deportation Cases* and *Predicted Prosecutions — Who Are They?*)

Schuk, Mykola — Ukrainian police collaborator accused by OSI of having "beaten and killed unarmed Jews and other civilians" during 1941-1944 period in Nazi-occupied Ukraine. Complaint filed February 8, 1983. Depositions taken in Soviet Union, July 1983. In pre-trial stage since fall 1983. Resides Allentown, Pa. Born Ukraine, 1909. (Schuk is also known as Mykola Zuk or Mike Shuk, and was first written about by Charles R. Allen, Jr. in 1978. Schuk was one of those cases developed by Allen during his 1978 testimony before U.S. Congress.)

Sokolov, Vladimir — **aka Vladimir Denisovich Samarin** (his real name) — Russian collaborator as Nazi "newspaper" editor, Oriel, RSFSR, responsible for anti-Semitic editorials urging genocide. Served as Gestapo informer. Faculty member, Yale University, 1959-1976. OSI complaint filed January 27, 1982. Still in pre-trial discovery. Resides New Haven, Conn., lives incognito elsewhere in New England and New York City. Born in U.S.S.R., 1913. (See *Predicted Prosecutions — Who Are They?*) Yale's professor Samarin was exposed in-depth first by Charles R. Allen, Jr. in major magazine/newspaper articles in 1976-1978. Allen discussed the Samarin case and Yale University's equivocating role therein during his 1978 testimony before U.S. Congress.

Sprogis, Elmars — Latvian Deputy Police Chief during Nazi occupation of that country. Charged June 23, 1982 by OSI with having "assisted the Nazis" in carrying out plunder of Jewish property and murders, as well as having "killed Soviet POWs (Prisoners of War)." Depositions taken in Latvia, November 1982. Trial commenced October 4, 1983 and completed October 11, 1983. May 1984, U.S. District Court Judge in New York ruled against OSI for not having sustained burden of proof. OSI "considering appeal" as of late 1984. Resides New York City area. Born Latvia, 1915.

Virkutis, Antanas — accused of carrying out "physical torture, abuse, starvation and executions" against civilian prisoners and "allied POWs from the U.S.S.R." from 1941-1944, as warden of Lithuanian prison under Nazis. OSI complaint filed March 14, 1983. Trial date not set, as of early 1985. Resides Chicago, Ill. area. Born Lithuania, 1913.

Deportation Cases

Artukovic, Andrija — accused of signing decrees, authorizing executions and persecutions of tens of thousands of Serbs, Gypsies, Jews and others, as Minister of Interior, Nazi puppet state of Croatia, 1941-1944. Order of deportation outstanding against him since 1952. Board of Immigration Appeals (BIA) decided in favor of OSI on July 1, 1981, revoking defendant's stay of deportation and ordering him deported. On appeal by defendant, Ninth Circuit Court of Appeals set aside BIA's decision that the accused mass murderer was amenable to deportation as was originally ordered in 1953. Ninth Circuit Court of Appeals ruled December 1, 1982 that U.S. Government must hold new hearing on Artukovic. March 21, 1983 that court denied OSI request for a rehearing, meaning whole case has to be retried and entire matter reverted. February 6, 1984, OSI filed motion to reopen hearings before BIA to argue that stay of deportation should be revoked. Resides behind armed walls in Surfside (Seal Beach), Calif. Born Yugoslavia, 1899. On November 14, 1984, Artukovic arrested after new extradition request by Yugoslavia. U.S. marshals and local police took Artukovic to detention facilities at University of Southern California Medical Center as defendant was "ailing." On November 27, 1984, federal court in Los Angeles denied bail. Croatian Information Service in Arcadia, Calif. dismissed actions as abetting "Communist propaganda and lies." Courtroom jammed with menacing Artukovic supporters, heavy security throughout federal center. One shouted at a Jewish spectator: "I am Ustashi! There are more of us than you and you will be dead!" Artukovic was remanded to prison (JTA, December 1, 1984). The Roman Catholic Cardinal Manning of Los Angeles on November 27, 1984 wrote in behalf of Artukovic saying that he had "for many years earned the respect of the priests of his Church and they are deeply concerned for his welfare." The mass murderer, Timothy Cardinal Manning suggested, was "innocent" of the charges against him, and voiced the "hope that (Artukovic) will merit the indulgence of the court."

Benkauskas, Henrikas — On March 25, 1984, OSI charged that Benkauskas "while serving in the Lithuanian *Schutzmannschaft* participated in the [shootings] of Lithuanian Jews in Kaunas (1941)...detained and murdered unarmed Jews, other civilians and Soviet [POWs] in the Minsk-Borisov-Slutsk area." Evidence indicates that Benkauskas was a member of the infamous Lithuanian 2nd Battalion commanded by a major war criminal, Antanas Impulevicius (see *The Lithuanian 2nd Battalion*).

Defendant had not yet replied to complaint, early 1985. Resides in Chicago, Ill. Born Lithuania, April 5, 1920.

Bernotas, Antanas — On July 8, 1983, the U.S. Justice Department sought this resident alien's deportation, charging that he took part in "the arrest, confinement, forced labor, beating/killing of Jews and suspected anti-Nazi political activists," as a Lithuanian Security Police officer during World War II. Evidence suggests Bernotas — under direction of SD (*Sicherheitsdienst*, SS intelligence) — worked with notorious Lithuanian 2nd Battalion (see *The Lithuanian 2nd Battalion*). In pre-trial stage since late 1984. Resides Hartford, Conn. area, age 76.

Demjanjuk, John — accused of assisting in extermination of tens of thousands of Jews, while guard with German SS in death camps at Sobibor and Treblinka, Poland. Denaturalization case filed August 25, 1977 and completed March 11, 1981. Ordered denaturalized, June 23, 1981. Appeals court affirmed denaturalization, June 8, 1982. Deportation action filed July 2, 1982. Defendant failed to appear for hearing. Tracked down and arrested by OSI, July 14, 1982; jailed until August 2, 1982, thus becoming first charged Nazi war criminal to serve a prison sentence in the United States. Deportation proceedings rescheduled for April 1983. Defendant refused to designate country to which he could be expelled, if found deportable. OSI named U.S.S.R. as that country. Deportation trial began April 11, 1983. After months of behind-the-scenes negotiations, Israel requested his extradition on November 18, 1983; on that day he was arrested. Demjanjuk bound over for hearing on Israel's request. He was set free on own recognizance, then placed on $50,000 bond. In May 1984, Demjanjuk was ruled amenable to deportation to the U.S.S.R. by U.S. Immigration Court. Such a ruling does not represent a government-to-government exchange. Demjanjuk's final deportation, therefore, remains unresolved. Demjanjuk is also the first Nazi war crimes suspect arrested under request for extradition. Resides Cleveland, Ohio. Born Ukraine, 1921.

Fedorenko, Feodor — accused of acts of persecution during service as armed guard at Treblinka. Denaturalization case filed August 15, 1977. Citizenship revoked by U.S. Supreme Court, January 21, 1981. First denaturalization to be ruled on by U.S. Supreme Court. Deportation complaint filed by OSI March 5, 1981. February 23, 1983, U.S. Immigration Court in Hartford, Connecticut ordered Fedorenko deported to U.S.S.R., finding specifically that he had "assist[ed] in thousands of murders" and had "demonstrat[ed] an immense lack of humanity." Defendant appealed March 8, 1983. Arguments heard August 29, 1983. April 1984, BIA upheld deportation order. After weeks of confusion and contradictory announcements, the OSI declared the Treblinka SS guard left the United States on Friday, December 21, 1984. According to Neal Sher, OSI director, "Fedorenko thus became the first war criminal to be deported by the U.S. to the U.S.S.R." No details were provided about the expulsion by the OSI. In fact, Fedorenko was found guilty of having concealed war crimes committed in Poland, not the Soviet Union. No mention of Poland's possible interest in Fedorenko was made. No comment was made by the U.S.S.R. Uninformed conjecture as to Fedorenko's fate characterized most of the press reports. The fact is that he was not returned to the soil on which he carried out his crimes. The record shows that Fedorenko visited on more than one occasion the Soviet Union as a tourist in the Ukraine. As early as 1978, the Soviet Union provided the Justice Department with documentation on Fedorenko. Moreover, several journalists (including Charles R. Allen, Jr.) secured in the 1970's authentic materials on Fedorenko's war criminal past. Allegations of intelligence usage of Fedorenko by both sides abounded in Washington on the eve of his departure. Resided Miami Beach, Florida, and "somewhere in Connecticut," age 76. Born Ukraine.

Hazners, Vilis — accused of atrocities against Jews of Riga while officer of Latvian "Self-Defense Group" (*Schutzmannschaft*), Nazi-controlled police unit. Hazners is an admitted erstwhile captain in the Latvian Waffen SS, a war criminal organization, per se. Case filed January 28, 1977 in Albany, N.Y. Judge ruled for defendant February 27, 1980. Oral argument by government on appeal presented September 4, 1980 to BIA. July 15, 1981, BIA dismissed OSI appeal outright. Since December 1983, OSI avowedly considering "various possible courses of action." Resides Dresden, N.Y. Born Latvia, 1906.

Kaminskas, Bronius — accused of participating in shooting of some 200 Jews and selection of some 400 Jews for execution in Lithuania. Case filed October 13, 1976, and adjourned indefinitely January 30, 1981, because of defendant's poor health. Must submit to periodic mental and physical examinations to determine fitness to stand trial. Resides Hartford, Conn., age 80. Born Lithuania.

Kisielaitis, Juozas — charged by the OSI on May 19, 1984 with having been a member of the Lithuanian *Schutzmannschaft* (see *The Lithuanian 2nd Battalion*) and with having "assisted in the arrest, detention and murder of civilians" in Lithuania and Byelorussia, 1941-42. Trial postponed on November 5, 1984. Resides Worcester, Mass. Born Lithuania, November 23, 1920.

Koziy Bohdan — On October 29, 1979, OSI filed denaturalization complaint against Koziy alleging he had concealed his participation in murders of defenseless civilians while he was a policeman at Lysiec, Ukraine, 1941-1942. On March 29, 1982, Koziy was ordered denaturalized. On February 27, 1984, the Eleventh Circuit of U.S. Court of Appeals upheld judgment of lower court. The higher court's ruling contained significant points: Koziy was found by both the trial judge and the Appeals Court to have personally murdered a young Jewish girl; to have murdered an entire Jewish family; and to have belonged to a criminally proscribed group, the Organization of Ukrainian Nationalists (OUN), a pro-Hitler movement in the Ukraine which to this day is active in various Ukrainian communities in the United States, Canada and Western Europe. Neal M. Sher, OSI director, stated on June 15, 1984: "The Court of Appeals dismissed Koziy's argument that the evidence from the Soviet Union had been improperly admitted...[the court held] that such evidence was fully permissible under U.S. law...that the findings were supported by the [Soviet] evidence." Deportation proceedings commenced summer 1984. Born Ukraine, 1923. Resident of Fort Lauderdale, Fla.

Kulle, Reinhold — accused of persecuting Jews, Poles, Russians and members of Jehovah's Witnesses, as SS guard leader at Gross-Rosen Concentration Camp in Silesia, August 1942 to January 1945. OSI filed complaint December 3, 1982. Defendant admitted at January 17, 1983 preliminary hearing that he was SS guard at the camp, but denied such "duty" provided grounds for deportation. Trial commenced in Chicago, August 10, 1983, and concluded November 1983. All briefs filed March 1984. Resident alien, born in Silesia, 1921; now a citizen of West Germany. Ordered deported to West Germany, November 20, 1984. Resides in Chicago, Ill.

Laipenieks, Edgars — Latvian security police official sentenced to death in 1962 *in absentia* for war crimes at Central Prison in Riga, where most victims were Latvian Jews. CIA agent since before 1950's. OSI filed deportation complaint June 2, 1981. At deportation hearings which took place January 26 - February 18, 1982, defendant admitted he had "beaten with [my] bare hands" "communist" prisoners in the Riga Prison, to "encourage them" to talk. June 9, 1982, Immigration Judge John C. Williams in San Diego, Calif., ruled Laipenieks not deportable. Fifteen months later, OSI appeal upheld by BIA, September 13, 1983, and defendant ordered deported. In most important decision since Fedorenko case, BIA found that Laipenieks had committed war crimes and carried out persecutions against Communists purely because of their political beliefs. Ruling added another dimension to previously held findings of American courts regarding persecution because of race, religion, and ethnic origins. A citizen of Chile, Laipenieks requested return to that country. September 19, 1983, Laipenieks filed appeal with U.S. Court of Appeals for Ninth Circuit. In a 2-to-1 ruling on Wednesday, January 9, 1985, the Ninth Circuit held the OSI had failed to sustain the burden of proof that Laipenieks persecuted Communist prisoners at the Central Prison because of their political beliefs. Judge Thomas Tang totally discounted the videotaped depositions by nine former prisoners under Laipenieks. The purpose of the Soviet government, wrote the jurist, "is to discredit émigrés who fled Eastern Europe at the end of the Second World War." Laipenieks's lawyer claimed that her client was only interested in locating those who committed "atrocities" against his family: "To the extent the Nazis were out doing other things, he was not personally involved with that [Nazis' other things]." OSI did not indicate its next steps but observers agreed that this reversal constitutes a major blow against the OSI's efforts. Resides San Diego, Calif. Born Latvia, 1914. (See *Predicted Prosecutions — Who Are They?*)

Lehmann, Alexander — Ukrainian deputy chief of police, charged with mass murder in OSI complaint filed November 23, 1981. Preliminary hearings commenced December 9, 1981; videotaped depositions taken in the Ukraine, summer 1982. Trial commenced fall 1983. February 27, 1984, Lehmann agreed to be deported to West Germany, of which he is a citizen. Ordered deported no later than May 26, 1984, but requested deportation withheld on health grounds. Health under ongoing review by government doctors, early 1985. Resides Cleveland, Ohio. Born Ukraine, 1919.

Linnas, Karl — accused of supervising and participating in execution of prisoners at concentration camp at Tartu, Estonia. At 1961 war crimes trial in Soviet Estonia, Linnas found guilty, sentenced to death *in absentia*. Denaturalization case filed by OSI November 29, 1979. Ordered stripped of citizenship by federal court July 30, 1981. Court specifically found that Linnas had personally taken part in "atrocities against men, women and children at the Tartu concentration camp." Linnas lost on appeal, January

25, 1982. OSI moved to deport him June 25, 1982. Decision to deport him rendered May 19, 1983. He appealed to BIA July 8, 1983. Deportation order upheld, August 1984. BIA sent case back to immigration judge to determine legality and propriety of deporting Linnas to Soviet Union in view of U.S. non-recognition of Soviet incorporation of Estonia (and Latvia and Lithuania). State Department concurred with OSI position that U.S. immigration law permits Linnas to be sent to any country willing to accept him. A "formal pleading" has been filed with Immigration Court (INS) in New York City. Commented OSI's Neal Sher on December 31, 1984: "[The Linnas decision] was a significant victory. To have taken a contrary position would have been tantamount to [the U.S.] government giving safe haven to one who had been adjudged by our courts to have been actively involved in persecution. Clearly, it was never the intent of our Baltic policy to protect Nazi persecutors." A brief uproar was touched off when it was revealed by the syndicated columnist, Jack Anderson, that ranking members of the U.S. Senate Foreign Relations Committee had been enlisted in an effort by a group of Ultra Right émigrées to block the deportation of the genocidist, Linnas. Former Republican Charles Percy of Illinois as well as New York Republican, Alfonse D'Amato, had intervened in behalf of the Nazi war criminal. In a hasty retreat, D'Amato claimed ignorance of the charges against his one-time constituent. Nathan Perlmutter, national director of the ADL, said D'Amato was "duped" and further defended D'Amato as "a friend of Israel" and "strong supporter" of the Soviet Jewry movement in the U.S. (The ADL also justified its featuring ex-CIA official, Ray S. Cline, who had rationalized utilization of Nazi war criminals on ABC's "Nightline" news program. See *Nazi Rocket 'Scientists,' Men on the Moon — and the CIA,* p. 49-52.) The émigré forces behind the maneuvering to enlist high political support for Linnas and other charged Nazi war criminals prosecuted by the OSI have been plying their Ultra Right wares for years. They derive largely from various subsidiary groupings of the so-called Assembly of Captive European Nations (ACEN), created in large measure with secret CIA funding in 1949. Linnas resides in Greenlawn, N.Y., age 64. (See *Predicted Prosecutions — Who Are They?*)

Maikovskis, Boleslavs — accused of murders of Jewish and other Latvian citizens and rounding-up of Gypies, while police chief in Rezekne, Latvia. Case filed December 20, 1976, and deportation hearings began October 1977. On January 9, 1981, BIA reversed immigration judge's decision, ruling that depositions may be taken in Soviet territories, and that their admissibility and evidentiary weight are to be determined by the immigration judge after they are taken. On January 21, 1981, immigration judge ordered depositions be taken in Latvia. Depositions taken there May 1981. On July 30, 1983, U.S. Immigration Judge Francis J. Lyons ruled defendant not deportable. OSI correctly reported that Judge Lyons "found that Maikovskis had indeed participated in mass arrests... at Audrini and in the burning of the village." The court also found that Maikovskis had "concealed his [SS-collaborator] police employment in order to procure a U.S. immigration visa." But Judge Lyons ruled Maikovskis' admitted involvement in persecution was not "adequately proved" and his admitted concealment of his Nazi past not "material"; nor did it rise to the "level of depravity" needed to make his alleged acts "contrary to human decency." Judge Lyons on July 30, 1983, ruled Maikovskis not deportable. After appeal by OSI, the BIA reversed Judge Lyons and ordered Maikovskis' deportation on August 13, 1984. The defendant has appealed the deportation. In 1965, Maikovskis was tried, found guilty and sentenced to death *in absentia* for war crimes in Latvia. Resides Mineola, N.Y. Born Latvia, 1904.

Palciauskas — OSI began deportation case on September 28, 1984. Trial set February 18, 1985. (See *Denaturalization Cases.*)

Paskevicius, Mecis — accused of murder of Jews and others while admittedly serving in Lithuanian Security Police. (See *The Lithuanian 2nd Battalion.*) Denaturalization case filed January 17, 1977; deportation case filed June 24, 1980. By consent judgment, U.S. District Court in Los Angeles on August 23, 1977, revoked citizenship. On December 16, 1980, found mentally incompetent to stand trial for deportation. Undergoes periodic mental and physical examinations to determine fitness to stand trial. Re-examined November 22, 1982 and found still unable to stand trial. Official residence, Los Angeles, Calif. Temporary residence, St. Petersburg, Fla., age 82.

Schellong, Conrad — accused of serving as company commander of several SS units in concentration camps and also training SS recruits at Dachau for concentration camp guard duty, *Schutzstaffel.* OSI filed complaint March 17, 1981. Trial commenced May 25, 1982 and concluded June 4. On September 7, 1982 judgment in favor of OSI. Citizenship revoked. Appeal in Circuit Court of Appeals, May 11, 1983, decided in favor of government, August 24, 1983. December 8, 1983, OSI filed deportation charges. Decision on appeal pending, September 1984. Resides Chicago, Ill. Born Dresden, Germany, 1910.

Theodorovich, George — OSI charged August 12, 1983 that defendant was a Ukrainian police collaborator in L'vov, Ukraine, 1942. He allegedly participated in "the persecution and murder of unarmed Jewish civilians" there. L'vov had been the scene of large mass murders under the Nazis and their collaborators. In his answer to the OSI complaint, Theodorovich admitted: "Yes, I was a candidate for police school in L'vov in 1942." Between December 1, 1983 and January 10, 1984, the one-time Ukrainian police officer disappeared from the Troy, New York area despite court orders for him to make official depositions. The case briefly attracted national headlines. Reporter Frank Dougherty of *The Philadelphia Daily News* tracked Theodorovich down in Philadelphia where he was living with his sister. Because of his actions in contempt of the law, Theodorovich was, on January 31, 1984, denaturalized. Deportation proceedings commenced in August 1984. Resides Philadelphia, Pa. Deportation proceedings held in Baltimore, Maryland, February 1985. Theodorovich's trial ended mid-March 1985. Decision awaited. At trial, court indicated defendant might well be sent to Argentina even if found guilty of having concealed his war crimes committed on the soil of the U.S.S.R. Born Poland, 1922.

Cases No Longer Active

Avdzej, John — charged by OSI with having concealed his Nazi past as German-appointed mayor 1941-1943 of Stolbcy, Byelorussia, a key town on railroad line between strategic cities of Minsk and Baranovici. Avdzej was a Nazi Fifth-Columnist. OSI had substantial evidence that Avdzej had "participated in the persecution of unarmed Jewish and Polish civilians" during the Nazi occupation of Stolbcy. He also helped to implement "the registration of Jewish inhabitants and their internment under inhumane conditions in the ghettoes" of that area. When confronted with OSI charges, Avdzej, in effect, conceded the government's case by consenting to leave the United States rather than face denaturalization/deportation proceedings. On January 5, 1984, the targeted defendant signed an agreement — under which he is barred from again entering the country — with the OSI. In February 1984 he left for West Germany where he now resides and surrendered his U.S. citizenship in Stuttgart on March 2, 1984. He had been naturalized in 1959. He had entered the U.S. under the DP Act of 1948; he said he was a farmer during World War II. Some sources have charged U.S. intelligence utilization of Avdzej *before* his naturalization. Avdzej was last a resident of Roselle Park, N.J. OSI director Neal Sher failed to return calls to inquiries as to possible West German prosecution of Avdzej. The Byelorussian was born in 1905.

von Bolschwing, Otto Albrecht Alfred — agent for Eichmann's office in the SS, Subsection IV-B-4 of RSHA (*Reichssicherheitshauptamt*), the Reich Central Security Office, Jewish Affairs, 1934-1941; agent of the SD (*Sicherheitsdienst*), SS Security/Espionage. Provided intelligence on Jewish organizations and leaders to prepare for deportations in implementing Final Solution. Born Germany, 1909. Entered SS 1932. SS# 353603. Entered U.S.A. in 1950's, naturalized, 1959. A major war criminal. Claimed he was double-agent for OSS during SD period. He was in fact a "contract agent" for the CIA, late 1940's-1960's. OSI filed denaturalization complaint May 27, 1981, after more than a year's investigation on West Coast and Europe. Voluntarily surrendered U.S. citizenship, December 22, 1981, admitting membership in Nazi Party, SS, and SD. Died in Sacramento, Calif., March 1982. All documents concerning his SS and alleged U.S. intelligence involvements have been sealed by the court. (Information on him secured and released by Charles R. Allen, Jr. *before* OSI filing.)

Dercacz, Mikhail — charged with beatings and executions of unarmed Jewish citizens in L'vov, Ukraine while police collaborator of SS, 1941-1943. Denaturalization case filed July 7, 1980. Summary denaturalization granted February 2, 1982. Defendant failed to file timely notice of appeal; deportation hearings set for August 12, 1983. Dercacz died August 8, 1983. Resided Queens, N.Y. Born Ukraine, 1909.

Detlavs, Karlis — accused of murder of unarmed civilians, primarily Jews, while serving as non-commissioned officer in Latvian Auxiliary Security Police, a collaborator organization. Case filed October 1, 1978. February 1980, immigration judge ruled in favor of defendant. OSI appealed decision to BIA, and argued appeal August 4, 1980. BIA dismissed OSI appeal October 15, 1981, holding that government did not establish materiality of defendant's misrepresentations by "clear, convincing, and unequivocal evidence." Detlavs died in Baltimore, Maryland July 22, 1983. Born Latvia, 1911.

Deutscher, Albert — Ukrainian accused of participating in mass murders as member of an indigenous fascist paramilitary unit there in 1942. OSI filed denaturalization complaint December 17, 1981; the next day, Deutscher, 61, a Chicago, Ill. resident, was killed by a train. The coroner ruled his death a suicide.

Hrusitzky, Anatoly — under an arrangement with the Justice Department, this Ukrainian war criminal left the country, an OSI announcement on July 8, 1984 stated. Month before accused had renounced his citizenship at the U.S. Embassy in Caracas, Venezuela. Hrusitzky came to the U.S. from Venezuela where he lived after World War II. (See *Deportation Cases*.)

Karklins, Talivaldis — accused of persecutions and murder in Madona, Latvia, while member of district police and commandant of Madona concentration camp, 1941-1942. Denaturalization case filed January 29, 1981. Trial had been set for March 15, 1983, but defendant died February 9, 1983 at age 68, in Monterey Park, Calif.

Kowalchuk, Mykola — OSI charged in complaint on January 13, 1977 that Kowalchuk had participated in persecutions while a Ukrainian policeman serving with Germans in Lubomyl, Poland, 1941-1942. A key eyewitness against him died before being deposed and a basic document "could not be located." OSI complaint withdrawn June 19, 1981. Born Poland, December 19, 1925. Lives in Philadelphia, Pa. (See *Kowalchuk, Sergei, Deportation Cases*.)

Lipschis, Hans J. — resident alien born November 7, 1919 in Lithuania. Citizen of West Germany. Admitted ten days before scheduled December 23, 1982 trial that he had been an SS-*Rottenfueher* (Corporal) in the SS-*Totenkopf Sturmbann* (SS-Death's Head Battalion) at the Auschwitz-Birkenau death camp. Also wanted for war crimes by the Allies in 1946. Did not contest deportation order. OSI noted in its October 24, 1983 Digest of Cases in Litigation that "on April 14, 1983, Lipschis' deportation was carried out, when he flew by commercial airliner to West Germany." OSI did not note that Lipschis successfully avoided both OSI and the FBI, used his own credit card for the flight, and was festively welcomed by family and friends upon arrival. OSI provided West Germany evidence, but nothing has yet been done about Lipschis' prosecution by the Federal Republic. Lipschis sent OSI a bill for his air fare, which OSI has vowed not to pay. Lipschis, OSI noted, "became the first person deported from the U.S. on Nazi war crimes charges in more than 30 years." (Actually in over 34 years.) Technically, he is the first person ever deported as a specific consequence of Nazi war criminal denaturalization/deportation proceedings that originated in 1972; and, in fact, the first to be deported under specific Nazi war crimes findings. (A 1950 case of an accused fascist collaborator was based on findings of "moral turpitude," having nothing to do with formal charges based on war crimes.)

Osidach, Wolodymir — accused of persecution and murder of Jews in the Ukraine while police officer and fascist collaborator. Denaturalization case filed November 20, 1979. Citizenship ordered revoked by U.S. District Court on March 17, 1981. Defendant filed notice of appeal on May 12, 1981, but died at age 76, on May 26, 1981, before motion was heard. Resided Philadelphia, Pa. and was discovered at a Ukrainian camp in Kerhonkson, New York. This camp also gave refuge to Osidach and other members of proscribed OUN (Organization of Ukrainian Nationalists), a notorious pro-Hitler organization.

Popczuk, Michael — Ukrainian policeman charged with persecution, beatings, forced labor of Jews in OSI denaturalization complaint filed June 28, 1983. Found shot to death eight days later at his home in Lynn, Mass., July 6, 1983. Death ruled as suicide, age 73. Born Ukraine.

Rudolph, Arthur — German rocket scientist naturalized under Project Paperclip program, managing engineer of the NASA Saturn 5 spaceship that took U.S. astronauts to the moon in 1969; who chose to leave the country in 1984 and surrender his citizenship rather than face OSI trial on his purported crimes against humanity during Nazi era (see *International Furor Over America's Use of Nazi War Criminals*).

Soobzokov, Tscherim — denaturalization case filed December 5, 1979, charging defendant had concealed past membership in proscribed Nazi military units including Waffen SS during World War II. He *denied* such membership on numerous occasions under oath. OSI director, Allan A. Ryan, on July 9, 1980 withdrew lawsuit against Soobzokov "with prejudice" because admissions originating with the CIA and State Department purportedly showed that Soobzokov had disclosed those very affiliations when he sought visa entry to the United States. Soobzokov had been used by the CIA overseas *before* his 1955 entry into the United States. Because of OSI's failure to file a broader complaint against Soobzokov, the elimination of the single charge of concealment enabled him to avoid further litigation under the OSI processes seeking denaturalization/deportation of alleged Nazi war criminals. Resides in Paterson, N.J. where he is a local leader of the Democratic Party. Soobzokov was born in 1918 (*not* 1923 as the OSI erroneously reports) in the North Caucasus, U.S.S.R. — (see section on *Predicted Prosecutions — Who Are They?)*

Trifa, Valerian aka Viorel Trifa. — Iron Guardist accused of persecuting Romanian Jews, inciting January 1941 pogroms in Bucharest and elsewhere in Romania. Denaturalization complaint filed by INS on May 16, 1975. After nearly five and a half years, Trifa consented to his own denaturalization. Deportation case began October 29, 1980. Trifa — using blatant delaying tactics that worked — then promptly appealed from his own consent decree revoking his citizenship on October 30, 1980. This move got Trifa another thirteen months as it took the Sixth Circuit Court of Appeals until November 3, 1981 to affirm his denaturalization. On May 17, 1982, the U.S. Supreme Court denied his attempt to start entire proceedings against him anew. Deportation hearings by INS court did not commence until October 4, 1982. After yet another attempt to delay, Trifa on October 7, 1982 conceded his own deportability in order to prevent full, officially documented evidence of his Nazi crimes from being placed on the court record. That day, Valerian Trifa was ordered deported; he was to be expelled within 60 days of the order. Trifa then filed an appeal to suspend deportation on May 29, 1984. (Trifa's efforts to gain entry into Switzerland, West Germany and Italy failed.) OSI then answered his appeal on June 8, 1984.

During this period, OSI sought to have Israel request the self-acknowledged pogromist's extradition to face trial in Israel. Pleading "insufficient evidence" to sustain a successful case, Israel declined to seek extradition. At OSI's request, the State Department routinely and with no apparent vigor, asked Romania (where he had earlier been accused of war crimes) if it desired to accept Trifa. Romania declined to demand Trifa be handed over for trial. (See *Deportations: When? How Many? To Where...?*) In December 1983, the OSI stated "efforts are now underway to locate a country that will receive [Trifa]."

The Archbishop of the Romanian Orthodox Episcopacy, the 70-year old Trifa, continued to reside at his Church's luxurious estate, the Vatra, at Grass Lake, Michigan, some 50 miles west of Detroit. More than a dozen Iron Guard veterans of the Holocaust have also resided there, as "priests," fully naturalized, since the early 1950's.

Thus by the summer of 1984, Archbishop Trifa had been able to use due process to delay for over nine years efforts by the U.S. government to expel him. During that time, Trifa's Nazi background was never put on the record in court.

Suddenly, on August 13, 1984, Trifa flew to Portugal under an order of deportation outstanding since October 7, 1982. Trifa had been living in the United States during the interim with a special identity card given him by OSI. By arrangement, Trifa had been given until October, 1984 — *not* the original 60 days from October 7, 1982 — to locate a country that would accept him. Moreover, it was learned after the fact of his departure, the OSI in a pre-arrangement with Trifa, delayed announcement of his leaving the country for 24 hours. Portugal, it was learned, had given him a 90-day visitor's visa, effective on August 13, 1984 but actually granted Trifa in December 1983.

The U.S. Justice Department declared its "mission" had been to deport Trifa, "and that has been accomplished." Major Jewish organizations hailed his departure and praised the Justice Department's "success." Some critics, however, decried what they saw as Trifa's "retirement to the sunny beaches of Portugal." Portugal then denied knowing Trifa was a notorious war criminal who had attracted international media attention for over a decade. In major Op-Ed articles, Charles R. Allen, Jr. revealed that both the State Department and Justice's OSI knew immediately about issuance of the Portuguese visa in December 1983 but had not said anything publicly. At the time OSI claimed they were still looking for a country to accept Trifa. A former OSI prosecutor, Eli M. Rosenbaum, conjectured that Trifa went to Portugal in order to get to Spain, where a large Iron Guard colony thrives. In August 1984, pressures in Portugal for the expulsion of Trifa were reported. *O'Jornal*, country's largest weekly, featured prominent stories from U.S. including extensive reprints of critical comment such as Allen's Op-Ed articles. On November 8, 1984, Reuters reported that Portugal had denied Trifa a residence permit, calling the Romanian "undesirable." The news-agency said that although Trifa faces expulsion, "it was not immediately clear which country will accept him." Said OSI's Neal Sher: "Trifa's departure is permanent. He cannot re-enter the United States." Mr. Sher did not return calls inquiring about further American interest in the Trifa matter.

Trucis, Arnolds — accused of persecuting Jews and others in 1941-1943 while member of Latvian Auxiliary Security Police and officer in SS Security Police. A Gestapo agent of SS *Sicherheitsdienst* (SD, Intelligence). Denaturalization complaint filed June 20, 1980. A leader of Daugavas Vanagi (Hawks of the Vanagi), a pro-Nazi Latvian organization in U.S.A. Defendant died December 6, 1981, before case brought to trial. Born Latvia, September 20, 1909.

Walus, Frank (Franciszek) — denaturalization case filed January 26, 1977. Defendant alleged to have been member of German Gestapo from 1940-1943; accused of having committed or participated in atrocities against civilians in Czestochowa and/or Kielce, Poland. Citizenship ordered revoked by Federal District Court, May 30, 1979. February 13, 1980, the Court of Appeals held that new evidence cast doubt on district court's decision. Court of Appeals vacated judgment and remanded case to district court for possible retrial, but OSI re-investigated and decided not to go forward with retrial. Purported new evidence, therefore, was never put to test of an actual trial. Post-WWII U.S. intelligence involvement is strongly indicated in Walus matter. Resides Chicago, Ill. Born Germany, July 19, 1922.

On January 1, 1985, OSI released its "Digest of Cases." The Artishenko case was listed as "Cases No Longer Active." It is clear that OSI and Artishenko struck a plea bargain: in exchange "for his cooperation and testimony in other investigations, the U.S. agreed not to commence deportation proceedings" against this admitted genocidist. The OSI also placed *Fedorenko* under "Cases No Longer Active" even though his curious "deportation" has been sharply criticised by knowledgeable sources. As in a growing number of OSI moves in 1984-1985, such moves have already shown OSI strategy to plea bargain and warehouse its final deportation cases while at the same moment claiming these cases as OSI victories (see *Deportations: When, How Many? To Where?*, p. 58 et seq.).

Predicted Prosecutions — Who Are They?

In the summer of 1979, Charles R. Allen, Jr. learned the identity of 37 major cases under review by the OSI. In many instances, their common characteristic was indication of formerly hidden U.S. government utilization. When Mr. Allen confronted the OSI with his list (based on his own investigations and analysis), the OSI refused comment.

Arranged alphabetically with brief descriptions, this list follows, containing the charges and allegations against these individuals reflected in the files of the OSI. An asterisk (*) after a name means government utilization is indicated. A double asterisk (**) means the OSI began prosecution *after the fact of Mr. Allen's listing*. (Data from Mr. Allen's copyrighted article written for the September 1979 *Jewish Veteran*. Jewish War Veterans of the U.S.A. decided editorially not to publish the list in their magazine so as not to preempt the OSI at the start of its work.) That list is published here in abridged, copyrighted form, as part of the historic record.

Bryzgys, Vincentas* — Roman Catholic Bishop, accused of collaboration and persecution of Jews in Lithuania. Ranking prelate in Chicago, Ill. today.

Caks, Raimunds* — Latvian journalist, Nazi propagandist during Nazi occupation of his homeland. Member of terrorist Perkonkrust (Thunder Cross). Residence, Milwaukee, Wis.

Cenkus, Stasys* — Top Lithuanian Gestapo agent as Chief, Lithuanian State Security Police. Member terrorist Iron Wolf. One of five top war criminals in U.S. Utilized by at least three U.S. intelligence agencies. Lived Howard Beach, Queens, N.Y. (Grandfather of professional tennis player, Vitas Gerulaitis, who himself has been quoted by the press as using anti-Semitic slander.) Died, 1982.

Dancis Augustus* — Latvian police collaborator and SD agent charged with murders in Alukene District, Latvia. Last known residence New York, N.Y.

Ernstons, Janis Arnold* — Former Latvian cleric, Gestapo agent, member terrorist Perkonkrust. Resides San Francisco, Calif.

Futala, Lew* — Ukrainian, member of anti-Semitic OUN (Organization of Ukrainian Nationalists). Charged with anti-Semitic acts as Nazi collaborator. Resides Yonkers, N.Y. where he is active in civic affairs and politics.

Hutyrczyk, Sergis* — Sentenced *in absentia* for crimes as concentration camp guard in Byelorussia, U.S.S.R. Resides New Brunswick, N.J.

Illing, Alexander R.* — Nazi collaborator as Ukrainian police chief. Resides Fresno, Calif.

Kairys, Liudas*,** — See section on *Who Are They? — Denaturalization Cases.*

Katkins, Zigurds* — Sentenced to death *in absentia* 1962 for war crimes as Latvian police official and Gestapo agent. Resides Boston, Mass. (since early 1950's).

Klimaitis (Klimavicius), Jonas*,** — See section on *Who Are They? — Denaturalization Cases.*

Koreh, Ferenc* — Hungarian lawyer, member of fascist Arrow/Cross Party, wrote anti-Semitic articles. Found guilty of Nazi collaboration, sentenced Budapest as war criminal to one and a half years imprisonment, five years loss of civil rights. Employed by Radio Free Europe. Resides Englewood, N.J.

Laipenieks, Edgars*,** — See section on *Who Are They? — Deportation Cases.*

Linnas, Karl*,** — See section on *Who Are They? — Deportation Cases.*

Mackevicius, Mecisiovas* — Lithuanian official of Nazi occupation charged with signing various genocidal decrees. Last known residence Chicago, Ill.

Macs, Edmund Gustav* — Latvian cleric charged with participation in deportations of Jews. Retired clergyman, resides Tacoma, Wash.

Nesaule, Peter* — Latvian cleric charged with collaboration as Gestapo agent. Employee of Radio Free Europe. Resides San Francisco, Calif.

Osidach, Wolodymir** — See section on *Who Are They? — Cases No Longer Active.*

Palciauskas, Kazys*,** — See section on *Who Are They? — Denaturalization Cases.*

Popov, Ivan* — Ukrainian police officer worked with *Einsatzgruppen D,* anti-Semitic murder squads. Poses as "John Nichols" in Miami, Fla. area.

Rabacs, Karlis* — Latvian journalist, Nazi collaborator now editing Latvian language newspaper in New York, N.Y.

Radchenko, Pavel F.* — Ukrainian police officer, extreme nationalist, charged with anti-Jewish "aktions." Last known residence (1960's) Cleveland, Ohio.

Samarin, Vladimir D.*,** (Listed as Sokolov) — See section on *Who Are They? — Denaturalization Cases.*

Sautins, Karlis* — Latvian cleric, Gestapo agent, Radio Free Europe employee in 1950's. Last known residence Cleveland, Ohio.

Schatoff, M.B.* — Former Red Army officer, Chief, Personal Security for Gen. Andrei Vlasov (hanged for treason, Moscow, 1946). "Vlasov Army" official wanted for war crimes in U.S.S.R. Member Columbia University faculty. "Consultant" with CIA and Pentagon. Longtime New York City resident.

Soobzokov, Tscherim*,** — In 1979 the OSI filed a complaint seeking his denaturalization for having allegedly concealed his past as a member of proscribed Nazi military units including the Waffen SS during World War II. OSI withdrew action "with prejudice" 1980. Utilization by intelligence agencies indicated. Local Democratic Party leader, resident, Paterson, N.J. See *Cases No Longer Active.*

Sterns, Alfreds* — Latvian police official, superior of Edgars Laipenieks (see above). Nazi collaborator. Self-admitted CIA agent, 1950's-1960's. Resided New York, N.Y. Deceased 1982.

Strughold, Hubertus* — World-famous physiologist, retired chief medical scientist U.S. Air Force. NASA (National Aeronautical and Space Administration) consultant. Charged with complicit knowledge of experiments on human beings at Dachau concentration camp while director of Nazi *Luftwaffe* (Air Force) Medical Research Center, Berlin. Resides San Antonio, Tex. OSI has five-year "open" file on Strughold.

Szulc, Johanna* — Guard and guard supervisor at several Nazi concentration camps. Resides New York, N.Y.

Trucis, Arnolds*,** — See section on *Who Are They? — Denaturalization Cases*.

Tulis, Peteris* — Latvian police official wanted for war crimes in U.S.S.R. Resides Philadelphia, Pa.

Wanko, Annemarie — Austrian physician and Nazi collaborator charged with experiments on camp prisoners. Resides New York, N.Y.

Warvariv, Constantine* — Charged with collaboration as Ukrainian employee of Nazi administration and SS in Rovno. Eyewitness testimonies place him working with SD unit there. Former high official of U.S. State Department, Washington, D.C. Deceased, April 6, 1982.

Woerner, Ottocar Anton* — Former Waffen SS officer charged with participation in atrocities on Eastern Front. Last known residence Lake Grove, N.Y.

Zakevicius, Stasys* — Official of Nazi puppet regime Lithuania. Signed various anti-Semitic decrees. Resides Los Angeles, Calif.

Zamuels, Voldemars* — Latvian police officer collaborated with *Einsatzgruppen A* forces in sweeps of Latvia. Resides New York, N.Y.

Zeltins, Teodors* — Latvian journalist, Nazi collaborator, founder of "The Anti-Semitic Institute" during German occupation of his homeland. Last reported (1985) in Milwaukee, Wis.

Did You Know That...?
Some Historic Facts, "Firsts" and Figures

- The first audio-visual testimony taken in the Soviet Union and Eastern Europe for use in U.S. federal courts originated with OSI trials. Such testimony has consistently been accepted by the nation's higher courts of review. At all times, the defendant's lawyer may, and does, examine and cross-examine video'ed eyewitnesses on the spot and all trial costs are borne by the U.S. government.

- OSI cases are civil, not criminal; yet the very court processes involving documentation, film footage and living eyewitness testimonies from survivors have enabled Americans often for the first time to observe actual living testimony in a court of law in their own country about the Holocaust and other crimes of Nazi Germany. The OSI trials, among other things, are a unique public education. However, attendance is often sparse.

- The first university course on the Nazi-war-criminals-in-America phenomenon was successfully launched in the 1984 winter-spring term at Tufts University by Dr. Jerry Meldon who combines dual expertise as a professor of chemical engineering along with his keen scholarship of the World War II period. Indeed, part of the basic syllabus of Dr. Meldon's course were *Nazi War Criminals Among Us* and *The Basic Handbook, Nazi War Criminals in America: Facts...Action* (including the entire of its bibliography, through the 2nd edition). The president of Tufts University, Dr. Jean Mayer, was a member of the French Resistance during World War II.

- Of the 43 cases brought to trial by late 1984, 21 of these individuals or 44% had first been uncovered and written about in depth by Charles R. Allen, Jr. (1963-1979).

- All documents and photographic evidence gathered and cooperatively given to the OSI by the justice ministries of such diverse nations as Great Britain, West Germany, France, Belgium, the Netherlands, Denmark, Poland, East Germany, Romania, the Soviet Union and Israel are first subjected to the rigorous tests of the hi-tech, scientific forensic labs of the FBI before being used in the American courts. In not a single instance has such evidence been shown to be other than authentic.

- The won-lost record of the OSI through 1984 stood at: 18 to 8 thus making the OSI probably the most successful 'law firm', in effect, in the U.S. government. Its average age (lawyers, researchers, historians, consultants, clerical/secretarial) is 36, making OSI one of the youngest on Capitol Hill. Moreover, its staff is made up of Irish Catholics, WASPs, Blacks, Jews and non-Jews — a genuine melting pot of American talent.

- Most of the cases brought before the U.S. courts are individuals who committed crimes in war-time Nazi-occupied Soviet Union and Eastern Europe. By 1985, their average age is 71.2 years, just above the mandatory retirement level in the United States. Most have been living here, however, for over 30 years, having come here at young, strong ages.

- Thus far no individuals charged with having committed their Nazi persecutions in Western Europe have been prosecuted. They are natives of Denmark, the Netherlands, Belgium, France, Italy, Spain, Norway and Great Britain. Evidence suggests that there are more than a few such persons here in the United States.

- Only 2 Germans have been charged before U.S. courts under the OSI processes. Yet available evidence shows that many individual German-born, Third Reich Nazis implicated in the persecutions of the Holocaust have long resided in the United States.

- Another related fact: Kapo is the term given to concentration camp/death camp inmates who were put over their fellow prisoners by the Nazi SS. Indeed Kapos had life-and-death powers. Some Kapos were decent; they helped whenever they could. However, many Kapos carried out daily brutalities against inmates. Kapos were often considered an especially odious breed of traitor. More than a few Jewish Kapos made their way to the United States after the Holocaust. The INS sought to deport three Jewish Kapos in the 1950's. Only one was actually ordered to be deported (to Poland). But his case dragged on until 1965 when it was dropped. Israel has severe laws governing Kapos found guilty of persecutions of camp inmates. To this day, there are more than a few Kapos living in the U.S., accused of having brutalized fellow Jews. OSI has open files on some of them, yet OSI is loathe to pursue such matters.

- A deported Nazi collects American social security benefits: fact or fiction? U.S. law provides 19 grounds for deportation. 18 carry immediate termination of social security benefits. Only one of the provisions *specifically exempts* the deportee from cutoff in benefits. It reads: "[Anyone deported] for activities conducted under the direction of or in association with the Nazi government of Germany during World War II" is *not* subject to termination of said benefits. This was an insurance clause for Project Paperclippers brought to U.S. The American Jewish Congress has protested this bizarre situation. Brooklyn, N.Y. Democrat, Charles Schumer, introduced a bill in the 1984 Congress which would end such preferential status (H.R. 4986). The Romanian war criminal, Archbishop Valerian Trifa, continues to receive his social security benefits while basking on the sunkissed shores of Portugal. Of the dozen or so charged war criminals who face deportation in 1984-1985, most will continue cashing checks under the law, as also do all accused Nazi criminals who are denaturalized before going to the deportation process.

- John Demjanjuk, aka "Ivan the Terrible," convicted of having hidden his past as an SS guard at the death camp, Treblinka, is the first accused Nazi war criminal actually hunted down, arrested and put in jail in the United States *after* the Holocaust. When ordered to appear for a deportation hearing in Cleveland, Ohio on July 2, 1982, Demjanjuk disappeared ten days later. OSI investigators tracked him down by July 14, 1982 and put him behind bars where he remained until August 2, 1982 when he was released to attend hearings leading to deportation. Demjanjuk is also the subject of the first, official extradition request since the OSI legal processes began in 1979. Israel wants "Ivan the Terrible," as he was called at Treblinka. The extradition case is a court action separate from the OSI trials.

The Lithuanian 2nd Battalion

One of the most efficient collaborator units in the Nazi killing machine was the 2nd Police Battalion of the Lithuanian national constabulary. Comprised in large part of volunteers and members of the fascist Iron Wolf, the unit operated directly under SS Police command, especially working with the mobile murder squads of *Einsatzgruppen B* and the *Wehrmacht* (Army). The 2nd Battalion figured prominently in the mass murders carried out against Soviet citizens in both Lithuania and Byelorussia, 1941-1943.

Its ultimate commander was one Antanas Impulevicius, aka Impulionis. In 1962 he was tried and sentenced to death *in absentia* for war crimes by a Soviet Lithuanian court. The U.S.S.R. also demanded that the U.S. extradite Impulevicius who had entered the United States where he was a naturalized citizen living in Philadelphia, Pa.

In his 1963 work, *Nazi War Criminals Among Us,* Charles R. Allen, Jr. detailed Impulevicius's life since becoming an American citizen. The accused war criminal boasted to Allen during the course of several interviews that "I am close to the FBI."

Allen also reported a curious fact: within a 10 square-block area of the Impulevicius residence in Philadelphia were then living some dozen alleged members of the 2nd Battalion once headed by Impulevicius.

By 1983-1984, some of these very individuals whose whereabouts had first been uncovered by Allen, were named in OSI denaturalization/deportation actions. Among them (alphabetically): Henrikas Benkauskas, Boleslavs Bogdanovs, Vitautus Gudauskas, Jurgis Juodis, Juozas Kisielaitis, Jonas Klimavicius, Juozas Kungys and Mecis Paskevicius, aka Mike Povilionis.

Allen investigated and wrote in-depth, face-to-face interviews in the 1960's with: Benkauskas, Bogdanovs, Kisielaitis, Paskevicius and Impulevicius himself, who died on December 4, 1970 in Philadelphia at age 63.

International Furor Over America's Use of Nazi War Criminals

1983-1984 witnessed three major revelations which directly and indirectly involved American utilization of Nazi war criminals after World War II. The following cases stirred an international furor which has not abated.

- **Robert Jan (Jean) Verbelen**

    A Flemish fascist as a youth, Verbelen was born in Belgium, April 15, 1911. Educated in Germany (1931-1933), he was a student leader of the pro-Hitler terrorist group, *Dervlag* (The Flag), during the 1930's in Belgium. He secretly joined the Nazi Party (NSDAP) in its AO (*Auslandsorganisation*), foreign or overseas party branches. A Fifth Columnist, he helped pave the way for 1940 Nazi invasion of his homeland. From 1940-1942, as an officer in para-military collaborator's unit, Verbelen recruited volunteers for the Waffen-SS Viking Division. He became an SS *Obersturmfuehrer* (1st Lt.) and later was promoted to the SD (SS intelligence). Specialist in counter-espionage directed at the Resistance movement in the Low Lands, especially against women underground fighters (1940-1945). Verbelen ran "nets" of informers and police spies, commanded terrorist sweeps of towns and villages in Flanders, carried out torture and killings of "suspected" Resistance fighters. During 1940-1942, Verbelen served in the SD with *Klaus Barbie* (see below) in hunting down anti-Nazis. Verbelen was "condemned to death" by a Resistance court even before the war ended. The charges included specific murders and torture for which Verbelen was allegedly responsible. He escaped with retreating Nazis, last reported in Austria in 1945.

    Reports and allegations of Verbelen's utilization by U.S. intelligence had appeared throughout Europe in the 1950's accompanied by attempts to extradite Verbelen for his war crimes in the Low Lands. Several books contained concrete details of his Nazi past.

    In 1983, the U.S. Army Intelligence & Security Command in Fort Meade, Maryland, released 92 pages of declassified Army and State Department documents on Verbelen to B'nai Brith's Anti-Defamation League in New York. Shortly thereafter the Army also released the same documents as well as additional materials to Charles R. Allen, Jr., special correspondent of the JTA *(Jewish Telegraphic Agency).*

The released "Top Secret" documents proved that Verbelen was picked up, possibly as early as 1945, by the 430th Detachment of the U.S. Army's CIC (Counter Intelligence Corps), part of the USFA (U.S. Forces, Austria), military occupational authority in Austria after the war.

Verbelen ran CIC "nets" of informers, police spies and provacateurs aimed at "Communist" and Soviet targets throughout Central Europe until late 1956. Analyses of the CIC documents by Allen showed unmistakably that Verbelen also worked closely with "V-Men" (espionage-sabotage agents) of the West German intelligence, the BND or Gehlen Org (so named after its chief, General Reinhard Gehlen, intelligence head of the Nazi army on the Eastern Front during World War II).

After the war, Gehlen surrendered to U.S. Army intelligence. He was set up in business by 1945-1946, under U.S. Army intelligence control. In 1948, the CIA took over the Gehlen operation completely. In 1956, as the BND, West Germany formally took over the Gehlen apparat. Gehlen remained its head until 1968.

Verbelen's networks of informers, spies and "rough" agents (that is, saboteurs/terrorists) included such fascist veterans of World War II as Iron Guardists from Romania, Arrow/Cross agents from Hungary and Ustashi assassins from Yugoslavia — all worked for the Nazis.

The evidence released in 1983 also suggests that Verbelen was probably operating under CIA control from the early 1950's through the early 1970's. When Verbelen left the CIC in 1956, he became an agent for the Austrian Secret Police. His role in 1950's-1960's, as a field "point-agent" for both West German and Austrian intelligence under the strategic direction (and financing) of the CIA is quite clear from the documented evidence.

In 1965, Verbelen was tried and acquitted for war crimes by an Austrian court which ruled that Verbelen, during his SD service in Belgium, was merely following superior orders. In 1985 he resides in Vienna. He holds Austrian citizenship.

The OSI was directed by the Attorney General of the U.S. to determine if Verbelen had ever visited the United States itself. The question of possible surreptitious, "privileged" entry at anytime into the country by Verbelen remains unanswered as the OSI has not responded with a report on this matter or to the specific queries put to it by Allen.

Klaus Barbie, U.S. Intelligence and the Catholic Church

- **Klaus Barbie, aka "Klaus Altmann," "Becker," "Mertens" et al.** — born, Bad Godesberg, Germany, Oct. 25, 1913. Joined Hitler Youth (HJ) at 19. Member Nazi Party (NSDAP), 1935, trained with Nazi Party intelligence, SD (*Sicherheitsdienst*). 1940 became 2nd Lt. in SD (SS *Untersturmfuehrer*). Early specialties: counter-espionage, "Liberalism and Pacifism," and "Rightist Movements." Developed "nets" of agents against targeted organizations, inseminated agents into them. As young SS, Barbie swept in with German army occupation of Low Lands (Holland, Belgium); stationed in Amsterdam. Responsible for tracking down "anti-Nazi tendencies" among Dutch people. Rising SD officer in Reich Main Security Office (RSHA) that combined SD with Gestapo and Kripo (criminal police). Barbie's service there from May 29, 1940 to late May 1942 suggests probable working relationship with *Verbelen* (see above).

  Nuremberg war crimes trial's evidence shows torture was routinely, widely and systematically used by RSHA agents.

  From May 1942 through early August 1944, Barbie stationed in Lyon, heart of French Resistance movements. Barbie's Kommando Lyon assignment: wipe out the Resistance. First, he served in SD VI (foreign intelligence); then to Gestapo (*Geheime Staats Polizei*, Secret Police), Section IV where he later became chief. Promoted to SS Captain *(Hauptsturmfuehrer)* November 1944. Last "heard of," according to U.S. intelligence, "in November-December 1944 in a hospital in Baden-Baden, Germany near French border." Klaus Barbie dropped from sight after late 1944. In 1949 he was reported living as a "businessman" in U.S.-Zone of Germany by the French press. Publicly, he was not spotted until a decade and some thousands of miles later in Latin America.

  Barbie was wanted by the Allies even before end of war. He was on Western Allies' CROWCASS lists (Central Registry of War Criminals and Security Suspects). He was on the U.N. War Crimes Commission's lists. The French charged him at 1947 and 1954 trials with war crimes ("torture of military personnel") and crimes against humanity ("murder of civilians," the deportation of 41 French orphans to Auschwitz, overall deportations of some 8,000 men, women and children; and 4,000 individual murders). Barbie sentenced to death *in absentia*, both trials.

(Curiously, the French did question Barbie in 1949 while he was in U.S. control but did not formally ask for his extradition.)

Barbie was particularly infamous for having allegedly tortured and murdered the celebrated French Resistance hero, Jean Moulin in 1943.

Official histories of the French Resistance record the torture techniques of the Lyon Gestapo under Klaus Barbie. To make prisoners talk: The Nazis used clubs, whips, screw-levered handcuffs that could be tightened until victim's flesh and bones were ripped apart. Hot needles shoved under fingernails. Acetaleyne blowtorches and electric wires attached to sexual parts of the body were used. Various forms of water torture, including drowning in a tub.

Reportedly, Barbie himself favored the "door torture." The suspected Resistant had his or her fingers forced between the hinges of the door and wall, according to an eyewitness survivor, while the door was open. "Then [the Gestapo] slammed the door shut, breaking his or her fingers and crushing them. Open and shut, open and shut, until blood gushed out of his or her hand like a fountain and he or she blacked out."

An imprisoned Resistant saw Jean Moulin after one of Barbie's torture sessions: "He was unconscious, his eyes dug in as though they had been punched through his head. An ugly blue wound scarred his temple. A mute rattle came out of his swollen lips." (Above citations taken from *Soldiers of the Night* by David Schoenbrun, New York, 1980, p. 288.)

When promoted to SS *Hauptsturmfuehrer*, the chief of the SS, Himmler himself, commended Barbie for his "untiring efforts in combatting resistance."

As early as the 1950's, European and Latin American journalists discovered Barbie in Bolivia where he had become a citizen. Under a series of military dictatorships, Barbie purportedly served as a "police" and "security" adviser to those regimes. French and West German extradition requests were rejected.

In 1972, the Paris-based "Nazi hunters," Beate and Serge Klarsfeld, spotlighted Barbie with on-the-spot demonstrations in La Paz, Bolivia calling for his extradition.

Then in 1982, the Bolivian dictatorship was overthrown. The situation had changed. Beate Klarsfeld in 1983 once more demonstrated in Bolivia. Again the French demanded Barbie be handed over. On February 4, 1983, Klaus Barbie was expelled from Bolivia. He landed in France hours later, charged with crimes against humanity.

Even before Barbie was flown to France, the world media featured stories claiming the Gestapo SS had been a secret American agent after the war; that he had been hidden from the French; and that U.S. intelligence helped him to get out of Europe.

Former CIC officers came forward and made such charges. BBC (British Broadcasting Corporation) TV aired allegations he had been a CIA agent as well.

In a long series for the JTA (See *What Background Material Is Available?*), Charles R. Allen, Jr., citing hitherto unrevealed U.S. government documents and allegations of former U.S. intelligence officers, offered additional evidence to corroborate further the overall accusations:

- that Barbie had been picked up and used by the U.S. CIC possibly as early as 1945-1946; possible initial involvement with British intelligence;
- that both the U.S. CIC and certain prelates of the Vatican helped him escape from postwar Europe;
- that the International Red Cross (IRC) supplied Barbie with bogus travel documents, abetting his escape;
- that Barbie was an active part of the 1945-1954 SS escape/terrorist organization, *Die Spinne* (The Spider) headed by the notorious SS Lt. Col. Otto Skorzeny, "Hitler's favorite Commando/SS";
- that Skorzeny was a self-confessed, documented CIA contract agent (i.e. not on CIA regular payroll) through the early 1970s, operating out of Madrid, Spain;
- that Barbie was a key organizer of a Nazi underground operating in early postwar Latin America;
- that Barbie was a sometime contract agent for the CIA in Latin America;
- and that Barbie had sometimes visited the United States, most significantly Fort Meade, Maryland, center of huge U.S. intelligence operations and para-military/counter-insurgency training.

The Allen/JTA series was carried world-wide in more than 400 newspapers and 24 languages.

ABC-TV's correspondent, John Martin, produced copies of original documents such as Barbie's entry visa into Bolivia showing that a Roman Catholic priest, Stefano Dragonovic, was his sponsor and copies of American immigration cards proving that Barbie had indeed visited the United States during the 1960's and '70's at Miami, Houston, San Francisco, Los Angeles bearing diplomatic visa privileges. ABC also publicized evidence that Barbie "stood at the center of a network of Nazis who bought and sold arms [and small tanks] in the world market... using a shipping company, Trans Maratina Boliviana, for the purchasing of armament[s]... sold to Israel." ABC also recounted Barbie's enterprises in counterfeit currency, American dollars and drugs.

John Martin also interviewed an Interior Ministry official of Bolivia who "says Barbie regularly passed information on Bolivian communists and Leftists to CIA contacts at the U.S. Embassy [at La Paz] using the Interior Ministry as an intermediary."

Against the background of a global media-upheaval, the U.S. Justice Department — after first dismissing Barbie as "only something of historical interest" (reported by Charles R. Allen, Jr., JTA, February 18, 1983) — reversed itself by directing OSI chief, Allan A. Ryan, to investigate possible American involvement in the Klaus Barbie matter.

Nearly six months later (August 16, 1983), Mr. Ryan released two volumes of history and analysis as well as more than 800 pages of declassified American intelligence and State Department documents called *Klaus Barbie and the U.S. Government.*

While critics were to fault some of the Ryan report, it nonetheless was the first detailed, documented admission by the U.S. government of utilization of a Nazi war criminal. Moreover, the claimed wholesale release of *all* intelligence documents used in the Ryan report was also an unusual step for any national government to take.

The report confirmed in telling detail virtually the entire of the already published media findings concerning Barbie. The use of what the CIC called "Rat Lines" to get Barbie out of Europe in 1951 via a "monastery route" originating in Bavaria, leading thence to Austria, dropping down south to Italy where Barbie was provided safe haven in Rome was revealed. Barbie exited Genoa by ship to Buenos Aires, Argentina on March 23, 1951.

The "Rat Line" used for Barbie in 1951 had earlier been employed by U.S. CIC in Austria. Shortly after the war a Croatian priest, Stefano Dragonovic, characterized by CIC as a "known...Fascist, war criminal, etc." ran that "Rat Line." He was also termed "unscrupulous in dealing with money," charging CIC $1,000 to $1,400 per escapee. (The same Dragonovic exposed by ABC, see above).

The Dragonovic evidence in the Ryan report strikingly confirmed Allen's series on the deployment of "monastery routes" for fleeing fascists and "defectors" by circles of Roman Catholic prelates. (See below *The Vatican-Nazi Connection — After the Holocaust.*)

The 1983 Ryan report took pains to deny CIA utilization of Barbie at any time. Its evidence to back such denial is not impressive while hard evidence of CIC agents who did participate in the Barbie flight from justice and then shortly thereafter became CIA agents in Europe is significant. Moreover, evidence unearthed in Bolivia by ABC's John Martin and Charles Allen's early findings of a CIA-Barbie linkage to the hunting down and killing of the guerrilla leader, Che Guevara, in Bolivia in 1967 are far more substantial than the Ryan report's contrary assertions.

The Ryan report recommended and got an official U.S. apology to France for having "obstructed justice" for not having turned Barbie over in 1947 for war crimes proceedings. The report also asserted *"no other suspected Nazi war criminal"* had been rescued by way of the "Rat Lines" as had Barbie. The report contended that there could be no criminal prosecution of American CIC agents who had prevented both the French and the U.S. State Department from learning of Barbie's whereabouts and use by CIC; the criminal statute had run out, the Ryan report stated.

The CIC officers, concluded the Ryan report, "[acted] to protect what they believed to be the interests of the U.S. Army and the U.S. government."

Nevertheless, said the report, no matter what "personal culpability" may have been involved under the "circumstances" of Barbie's employment and escape, the "U.S. government cannot disclaim responsibility for their [CIC agents] actions."

Klaus Barbie at this writing (April 1985) remains in a French prison awaiting trial, reportedly scheduled for spring 1985. Informed opinion envisions a 1985-1986 trial.

"A Pact with the Devil"

● An editorial response in the August 18, 1983 *The Miami Herald* reflected much of the criticism of the Justice Department's conclusions: "The Justice Department says that the statute of limitations for obstruction of justice expired...and so no prosecution of [two yet living] men responsible is possible. Nonsense. No statute of limitations protects war criminals, and no statute of limitation should be permitted to protect those who aid and abet the escape from justice by war criminals.

"The obsession to oppose communism at any cost led six U.S. Army officials to make a pact with the devil — Klaus Barbie. The American conscience that today is repulsed by that fact also should stand alerted, for the kind of thinking that led to it remains dangerously common in America today."

The La Vista Report and The Vatican-Nazi Connection: 'Rat Lines'... 'Monastery Routes'

A "Top Secret" U.S. State Department report, dated May 15, 1947 — the product of nearly two years of deep undercover investigations throughout Europe — concluded that "the Vatican is the largest single organization involved in the illegal movements of emigrants," including wanted Nazi war criminals and collaborators.

This extraordinary report was authored by a highly specialized intelligence operative, Vincent LaVista, then 40 years old; he died in 1951 while on way to an assignment in the Far East for the CIA.

Through other "Top Secret" State Department documents it was established that LaVista had on June 15, 1945 been posted to the American embassy in Rome "for special duty as a Safe Haven agent" though innocuously listed as a "military attaché."

Operation Safe Haven was a vast counter-intelligence effort mounted by the United States government at its highest levels to ferret out, track down and prevent the flight from Europe of capital, currencies, and other tangible fiscal assets held by ranking Nazis.

LaVista's assignment was to uncover any Nazi attempts to smuggle capital out of occupied Europe by way of Italy. It was considered one of the

---

No Nazis Imported, Asserts OSI Head

• The following is excerpted from an interview with Allan A. Ryan Jr., then director, Office of Special Investigations (OSI), by Ralph Blumenthal of *The New York Times* (July 16, 1983):

Q. Have you found any cases at all in which people who committed atrocities were knowingly let into the country for intelligence purposes?

A. (By Mr. Ryan) No. Maybe one, but it was unclear. He was later deported, back in the 50's. The others came in perfectly ordinary ways.

most strategically important intelligence assignments of the post-war decade. The U.S. government feared that such Nazis would regroup in Latin America in order to establish "areas of influence;" and, with enormous financial and capital resources, mount serious attempts to return to power in a resurgent Germany.

Thus the assignment of LaVista as a Safe Haven agent was a very high level move by the United States. There were other Safe Haven agents throughout Europe, the historical record shows, including Soviet-occupied Germany and newly communist Eastern Europe. (All such operations were ultimately incorporated into the CIA.)

The "LaVista Report" was a tightly restricted document that circulated only at the very top of American policymakers. The U.S. Secretary of State, the White House and Ambassadorial rank were its sole initial (1947) distributions. It listed 22 "relief and welfare organizations" operating under the control of the Vatican. These "welfare agencies" or "refugee bureaus," gave aid and assistance to scores of thousands of quite authentic refugees, including Jews, who for whatever reasons were fleeing Europe to start homelands elsewhere. Estimates of Europe's postwar refugees range as high as 8 million. Among them, however, were also an undetermined number of wanted Nazi war criminals who used the same "monastery routes" — sometimes cheek by jowl with Jewish refugees; and with the assistance of certain prelates who were directing those 22 "welfare organizations" which, according to the LaVista Report, "enjoyed the protection of the Vatican."

The LaVista Report listed in detail the names, addresses, telephone numbers and daily organizational habits of those prelates — among them bishops, monsignors, priests and monks — who specifically provided aid in provable instances for escaping Nazis ranging from well-known individuals to groups of SS officers on the run.

The LaVista investigation inseminated its own agents, posing as refugees, who actually travelled over the "monastery routes," meticulously documenting their reports.

The report concluded that "The Vatican's justification of this illegal traffic is simply the propagation of the Faith."

In another related "Top Secret" State Department memorandum, it was reported that "...in countries where the Church is a controlling or dominating factor, the Vatican has brought pressure to bear which has resulted in the foreign missions of these Latin American countries taking an attitude of almost favoring the entry into their country of former Nazis and former Fascists or other political groups so long as they are anti-Communist."

At the very time that the State Department was preparing an internal "action program" of its own to implement the suggested remedies in the LaVista Report, the U.S. Army's CIC was already using Klaus Barbie, Robert Jean Verbelen and other similar Nazi ilk (see above, and references among listings of denaturalization/deportation cases).

Within less than four years, Barbie himself would be a primary beneficiary of these very "illegal emigration routes" by one of the 22 "welfare units" documented in the LaVista Report. (The reader will recall that the CIC dubbed these routes "Rat Lines.")

In point of fact, the LaVista Report demonstrated, by inseminating its agents, for example, along the Hungarian route, just how a wanted Hungarian Nazi was able to: get out of Europe with both Vatican and American help; and secure American government assistance in order to enter the United States.

This illustrative case concerned one Ferenc Vajta (spelled as "Vajhta" in the 1947 LaVista Report). In Appendix D, p. 5, LaVista noted: "The first Hungarians escaping from the [Communist] Government's repressive measures...are now arriving illegally in Italy." They were considered "rebellious," stated LaVista, and "supposedly" were planning a coup to overthrow the Hungarian government.

He said: "The Hungarians are also trying to hunt down the Hungarian fascist, Vajhta Ferenc, who, so their propaganda says, is living in great state at the 'Grand Hotel,' Rome, under the very eyes of the Anglo-American authorities. However, VAJHTA is not at the Grand Hotel but, according to fairly reliable sources, in one of the many monasteries in the Rome area" (original emphasis).

LaVista noted too in 1947 that the Hungarians were seeking Vajta's extradition for war crimes through "the Italian police."

Nearly 37 years later (Feb. 23, 1984) *The New York Times* reported that "In Dec. 1947...Vajta, who had been an aide to Ferenc Szalasi, the executed Hungarian Nazi leader, was discovered living in New York. A Congressional inquiry determined he had entered the United States on a diplomatic visa issued by the American consul in Madrid."

The Times did not have enough facts to report the salient essentials of the Vajta case and its relationship to the LaVista Report, the Vatican and U.S. intelligence utilization of wanted Nazi war criminals.

Here are those essential facts:

- Vajta was a young leader of the Hungarian Arrow/Cross, a terrorist gang and fascist party. He was later described in American CIC classified reports as: "a Hungarian war criminal," a "100% pro-Nazi" and "absolutely without a trace of decency."

- The editor of an Arrow/Cross publication, Vajta was a close colleague of Ferenc Szalasi, leader of Arrow/Cross. Szalasi directed anti-Semitic mass murders while collaborating with Nazi Germany. The Arrow/Cross party was proscribed by the U.N.'s International Refugee Organization (IRO) which ruled that "any members of Arrow/Cross are outside the mandate of the IRO." This meant that they were subject to automatic arrest, were to be handed over to the Hungarians for war crimes and were in no way to be treated as *bona fide* refugees.

- From October 1944 to May 1945, Vajta was the Arrow/Cross consul in Vienna, appointed directly by Szalasi.

- Vajta was captured and interrogated by the American Office of Strategic Services (OSS), famed wartime intelligence. The OSS recommended to the U.S. Army's CIC that Vajta be handed over to the Hungarians (who already had made such a request).

- Vajta somehow escaped custody. He landed in French-occupied Austria. In exchange for his liberty, Vajta directed French intelligence to a hidden Nazi cache of diamonds and gold — some counterfeit — allegedly worth $7 million in 1946. In return, the French secreted Vajta into Italy in August 1946 even while the American embassy in Rome — acting already at that time in response to LaVista's earlier findings regarding Vajta and other Hungarian fascists in Italy — was itself looking for Vajta! (In a sense it was a reverse Klaus Barbie case; this time French intelligence was keeping its Nazi, Vajta, from the Americans.)

- The precise details of how American CIC picked up Vajta and "carded" (put him on the payroll) the "Hungarian war criminal" are not known but at the latest he was made a CIC agent *in Italy* in spring 1947 (about the same time LaVista's final "Top Secret" memorandum was finished and circulating).

- By summer 1947, the Italian police were closing in on Vajta so as to capture him and hand him over to the Hungarians.

- Vajta disappeared and then shortly materialized in Madrid, Spain by way of the Genoa exit port described by LaVista. From there, Vajta, partly on the strength of a CIC letter of recommendation, secured a 6-month tourist visa from the American embassy and went to New York in December 1947. His self-declared "mission": to organize a contingent of Hungarian "Freedom Fighters" to overthrow the communist regime of Hungary.

Vajta was soon detected by anti-Nazi Hungarians in the United States. They tipped off the media. On January 4, 1948, the network radio broadcaster, Walter Winchell (who early exposed the presence of Nazi war criminals in the country), tore the mask off Vajta and lambasted the State Department's "shameful, disgusting conduct" in the case.

After his trial before an INS judge, Vajta was ordered expelled and remanded to Ellis Island. In 1951, Vajta was deported to Colombia — not to communist Hungary where he committed his crimes and was wanted for both war crimes and treason. In Latin America, Vajta lived out his years as an economics teacher at a Catholic university in Bogata. Vajta was the only Nazi war criminal deported from the United States before 1983. Moreover, Vajta was deported on the grounds of "moral turpitude," not because of his past as a Nazi war criminal.

Vajta died peacefully sometime in the late 1960's in Columbia and was accorded last rites by the Church.

Besides Barbie and Vajta, other wanted major Nazi war criminals also successfully availed themselves of the "Vatican routes" and/or U.S. intelligence utilization. Some of the "illegals" who fled via the "Vatican routes" first revealed in detail by the 1947 LaVista Report are shown in the chart on page 48.

Proponents and officials of the Roman Catholic Church have been quick to point out Vatican relief agencies did in fact aid scores of thousands of legitimate refugees. And such is the fact. Moreover, these advocates also insist that even though individual clerics may have been involved in assisting Nazi war criminals in their escape from justice, there is no hard evidence — including what makes up the LaVista Report and its ancillary materials — that these priests acted with the approval of the Vatican, and, therefore, Pope Pius XII who has been the object of much criticism for not having spoken out against Nazi Germany's genocides against the Jews and other millions of victims.

During 1983 and midway through 1984, global media response to the Allen materials on the LaVista Report and the "Vatican routes" reached an estimated global audience of 1 billion (starting with the JTA and *Reform Judaism* 1983-1984 series, then *The New York Times* front-page stories beginning on Jan. 26, 1984 through subsequent Op-Ed pieces by Allen).

Official reaction to Allen's findings by the Vatican was initially characterized by such remarks as: "Absurd, absolutely" (Rev. Pierfranco Pastore, deputy Vatican spokesman in Rome to Associated Press, June 19, 1983); "It doesn't even merit a denial," Vatican spokesman to Reuter's wire services (same date); "They [LaVista's findings] are nothing but air.... Probably another hoax, another Hitler Diaries!"

After the U.S. State Department, U.S. National Archives and the U.S. Justice Department confirmed the authenticity of the LaVista Report and Allen's account of the document, there was a perceptible change in the Vatican's remarks as the controversy grew.

On Feb. 5, 1984, Father Robert Graham, a venerable Vatican authority on the Church and the Holocaust — regarded by knowledgeable observers as among the finest intelligence analysts of the Vatican since before World War II — met with Charles R. Allen, Jr. over an hour-long NBC radio network program ("The Al Angeloro Show") in what some critics called "a positive, rational dialogue." Father Graham agreed with Allen that some of the LaVista documents "ought to be searched for in our own archives."

On the program, Allen described in detail State Department documents showing that the deputy to President Harry S. Truman's Special Envoy to His Holiness the Pope, Myron C. Taylor, had met on July 27, 1947, with Mons. Walter Carroll, Secretariat of the Holy See in charge of Vatican banking and an intimate of Pius XII. At their meeting, the American diplomat conveyed official concern in an "oral message" over communist infiltration of the welfare agencies' routes and, by implication, wanted Nazi criminals. Mons. Carroll was quoted by the American envoy as denying any "Vatican connection" with the "agencies mentioned in LaVista's report."

Significantly, the diplomat said he did *not* press Mons. Carroll on how the illegal routes were financed because of "Vatican sensitiveness over the amount of *American private capital which has gone into the financing of illegal emigration"* (emphasis added).

Father Robert Graham stated on the NBC network radio program to Allen that "we ought to see what's in our own archives on that because I don't know anything about such a meeting. Interesting."

Allen also contributed an Op-Ed article to *The National Catholic Reporter* (March 2, 1984), engaging in an exchange with Mons. John M.

Oesterreicher, Catholic expert on Judaica studies at Seton Hall University. Over the articles ran an eight-column headline: "Debate Rages: Did Vatican...Help Nazis to Escape from Europe?"

At the original suggestion of Allen and the magazine *Reform Judaism,* leading organizations and individuals from both the Jewish and Roman Catholic communities are currently exploring some form of inquiry into the questions and implications raised by the LaVista Report and its contents.

On CBS-TV Network "Morning News" shortly after *The New York Times* ran its front-page story, Mr. Allen told millions of viewers: "This is not the time for any kind of rancor or baiting. It's the time for both of these great faiths to sit down together, search for the fuller truths and, in a spirit of positive, mutual cooperation arrive at those truths so as to advance the ecumenism everyone wishes."

By late February 1984 (see *The New York Times*, Feb. 23rd), press reports appeared that "Jewish organizations hoped to arrange a meeting with Vatican representatives in Amsterdam to discuss an inquiry into such allegations" contained in the writings of Allen and the Klarsfelds about the Vatican in the post-Holocaust period.

No reports eminating from Church sources had been recorded by early 1985.

Some of the Illegals, 1945 - 1950's*

Name	Charges	Escape Routes	Exit	Sponsor	Remarks
Klaus Barbie "Butcher of Lyons"	12,000 deportations, murders French Resistance fighters	U.S. CIC "Rat Line" 1951, West Germany, Austria, Italy; Argentina, Bolivia	Genoa, Italy 1951	Padre S. Dragonovic, Rome, Italy (Bolivian visa signed by Barbie)	Dragonovic was identified as the operator of Genoa exit by a priest called a "Vatican representative" in LaVista Report.
Adolf Eichmann	SS "desk" murderer, ran logistics of Holocaust	1950: West Germany, Austria, Italy, Argentina	Genoa, 7/14 (Arrived Buenos Aires, August 1950)	Israel's prosecutor wrote that Eichmann stayed at "a monastery in Genoa" where "a Franciscan monk provided Eichmann with a [International Red Cross] refugee passport [travel document] bearing the name Ricardo Klement." (The alias given by the monk to Eichmann and used by Eichmann while in Argentina before his capture and trial.) In 1956, Eichmann's fourth son was "christened Ricardo Francisco, Ricardo after himself and Francisco after the Franciscan priest in Genoa who had provided the passport to Argentina" (*Justice in Jerusalem* by Gideon Hausner, N.Y. 1968, pp. 271-272).	Eichmann was hanged 1962 in Israel for war crimes.
Ante Pavelic "Hangman of Croatia"	600,000 murders of Croats, Serbs and Jews, Nazi-occupied Yugoslavia	1945: Yugoslavia, U.S. occupied Germany, Italy, Spain, Argentina	Genoa, 1947 or 1948	Not Known	Both U.S. and Yugoslav intelligence reported Pavelic was disguised as "monk" on arrival in Argentina, accompanied by "other monks" (Ustashi war criminals). All carried IRC passports.
Walter Rauff	SS commander, gas vans East Front, 1941-1943 killings of 97,000 Soviet Jews	1949: escaped U.S. POW camps; West Germany, Austria, Italy, Rome; Syria, Argentina, Chile	Genoa to Syria	LaVista and several authorities named "Bishop (Alois) Hudal's organization"	Rauff himself wrote of "aid" he received from "two priests" in Rome and of living "securely" in Rome "monasteries" before exiting Genoa. Rauff escaped from SS prison camp Rimini 1946 (detailed by the LaVista Report; Rauff, however, *not* named in LaVista). In Dec. 1962 sworn statement before Supreme Court of Chile (considering West German extradition request for Rauff), the SS genocidist swore: "With the help of the Catholic Church, my family...escaped from Russian-occupied Germany" and reunited with Rauff in Rome monastery. Rauff died peacefully in Chile, 1984.
Eduard Roschmann "Butcher of Riga"	Commandant, Riga Ghetto during Holocaust	1948: U.S.-occupied Germany, Austria, Italy, Argentina, Paraguay	Genoa	Not Known	Potsdam War Crimes Doc. Center, GDR, claims documents show escape via "monastery routes."
Franz Stangl	Commandant, Treblinka death camp	Austria, Italy, Syria, Brazil	Genoa, 1948	Stangl himself named Bishop Hudal	Stangl detailed aid received in Vatican City, including IRC passport and visas.

*Compiled and edited by Charles R. Allen, Jr. for his series "The Vatican and the Nazis: The LaVista Report," Spring-Summer, Fall, Winter, 1983-1984 (Vol. XI, No. 4; Vol. XII, No. 1; Vol. XII, No. 2. *Reform Judaism*; Union of American Hebrew Congregations, with kind permission.) Copyright © Charles R. Allen, Jr., 1984, 1985.

Nazi Rocket 'Scientists,' Men on the Moon — and the CIA

More revelations about high level intelligence usage of war criminals were running headlines through the mid-1980's as the following major developments demonstrated.

Rudolph, Dr. Arthur L.H. — German rocket engineer, born 1907. Early training in rocketry engineering. Joined Nazi Party 1931. (Berlin Documents Center lists a "Dr. Arthur Rudolph born in 1904, NSDAP #193418 [with appointment as an] SS captain, April 20, 1940." It should be recalled that it was not unusual for German scientists, educators and other professionals to hold SS officer appointments. For example, Werner von Braun, the so-called "Father of American Space Flight," held SS membership and officer's rank. See p. 57.)

Rudolph was a prominent technician in the German V-1 and V-2 rocket programs during World War II. He was production manager for the V-2 rockets from 1943-1945 at underground factory located in the Harz Mountains of eastern Germany; V-1 and V-2 stand for *Vergeltungswaffen* (reprisal/revenge weapons). That site used slave laborers from the Dora-Nordhausen complex called by SS and concentration camp prisoners alike "a hell worse than Auschwitz."

Most of Dora's some 60,000 prisoners were forced to work under indescribable conditions in the labyrinthine tunnels which often plunged 1400 feet under the mountains. Many inmates had been members of Europe's Resistance movements. An estimated 30,000 prisoners perished there; many by shooting, garroting and mass hangings. The SS literally whipped the inmates to work 14-hour shifts, 7 days-a-week.

Rudolph escaped from Soviet-occupied Germany in 1945 to the U.S.-Zone. There he was recruited by Project Paperclip which ultimately brought 1,558 German and Austrian scientists, technicians and "intelligence resources" to the United States. They were employed both by the Pentagon and corporate military contractors.

Rudolph was contracted for use by U.S. Army's Ordnance department where he immediately joined von Braun and other rocket engineers to work on the American rocket/missile program.

Rudolph was, from 1951-1961, project director of the Army's Redstone and Pershing missile programs. Then he became the supervisory chief engineer of the Saturn 5 rocket — the largest ever constructed and the ship which carried men to the moon in 1969.

For his work on Saturn 5 — Rudolph was not an aerospace scientist, as he has been popularly characterized — the naturalized (in 1954) technician received the Distinguished Service Medal, the highest honor of NASA (National Aeronautics & Space Agency), in 1969. He retired that year and became a highly paid consultant to an aerospace corporation in San Jose, Calif. He left government employ with a lucrative pension, medals, honors and full social security benefits.

Because of the diligence of a young OSI prosecutor, Eli M. Rosenbaum, the full background of Rudolph was, by 1983, ascertained. Working on his own time and weekends, the Harvard Law graduate pieced together the facts of Rudolph's complicity in the employment of slave labor at Dora-Nordhausen.

"With the full knowledge of the grotesquely inhumane conditions [at Dora], Rudolph personally participated in the procurement of concentration camp inmates to serve as slave laborers and, while working under [Rudolph's] supervision, inmates perished in large numbers," Mr. Rosenbaum told *The New York Times'* Ralph Blumenthal, whose October 18, 1984 story broke the case worldwide.

When confronted by the OSI with its documented charges, Rudolph signed an agreement with the Justice Department on November 28, 1983. By its terms, he was to depart the United States rather than contest the charges against him at a denaturalization trial.

On March 27, 1984, Rudolph quietly left for West Germany. On May 25, 1984, he surrendered his citizenship certificate to U.S. consular officials at Stuttgart, West Germany. On October 17, 1984, OSI director, Neal Sher, announced Rudolph's departure and loss of U.S. citizenship.

There has never been an explanation as to why the Justice Department waited for nearly a full year before revealing the Rudolph matter.

The New York Times (Oct. 18, 1984) reported that "investigators said the State Department had hesitated to approve Mr. Rudolph's surrender of his citizenship."

Follow-up attempts by this writer and other journalists to clarify the puzzling delays in the Rudolph case were rebuffed by the State Department. OSI's Sher did not return telephone calls which had specified the nature of the inquiries.

In subsequent FOIA (Freedom of Information Act) requests by Mr. Blumenthal, it was learned through released declassified intelligence documents that Rudolph had been initially categorized as "an ardent... 100 percent Nazi" who was "dangerous" and a "security threat" who should be detained (*The New York Times*, Nov. 8, 1984).

Nonetheless, in 1945, Rudolph was admitted to the United States under Project Paperclip, a huge American intelligence undertaking combining State Department/Pentagon/Intelligence/Commerce Department forces.

Then on March 4, 1946, the Army revised its own original estimate. Rudolph was "not a war criminal" but was "an ardent Nazi," the Army decided.

Yet a further "revised security report" was issued on Rudolph two and a half years later (September 27, 1948). The Nazi rocket engineer was now "not an ardent Nazi."

The same FOIA documents released to Mr. Blumenthal contained a June 13, 1945 report noting that Rudolph, in addition to his 1931 enlistment into the Nazi Party, was a member of the SA (*Sturmabteilungen*) or Storm Troops of the Nazi Party.

Under "remarks" on this report (titled a "qualification sheet for German scientific personnel" under Project Paperclip) was a hand-written notation: "100 percent Nazi, dangerous type, security threat. Had to leave SA in 1934. (*Oberscharfuehrer*, sergeant)...suggest internment."

No explanations were given for these reversals or failure to carry out the internment of Rudolph.

Another intelligence report (possibly British in origin, *The Times* surmised) stated that a suspected war criminal "May be wanted in connection with Dr. Rudolph's activity in Mittelwerke [i.e. Dora-Nordhausen rocket factory] where foreign labour was emp[loyed] and mistreated."

In 1947 at a CIC interrogation, Rudolph first claimed that "working conditions [at Dora] appeared good." When pressed, Rudolph admitted they were "bad."

He at first denied seeing any punishment of prisoners. He saw no killings in the Dora tunnels. Again he was prodded. This time about mass hangings in 1944.

A survivor of Dora described exactly such hangings:

"An electric crane in the tunnel lifted 12 prisoners at a time, hands tied behind their backs, a piece of wood in their mouths, hung by a length of wire attached at the back of their necks to prevent crying out. All...had to watch these mass hangings" (*Dora* by Jean Michel, 1979, p. 96).

Rudolph then confessed: he had been there.

A German official at Dora further implicated Rudolph. At the same 1947 interrogation, this official swore:

"[Rudolph] told me that the men would be hanging there the last six hours of one work shift and the first six hours of the next work shift so that the Germans and *Haftlinge* [prisoners] could see."

When confronted by this allegation, Rudolph said he could not remember the exchange.

Even after arriving in West Germany in 1984, Rudolph continued to deny all charges against him, calling them "lies, of course." He has since applied for West German citizenship. West German legal sources doubt there will be a move to prosecute Rudolph since any act short of murder is not actionable because of the country's statute of limitations on "lesser" war crimes/offenses.

In a 1953 statement to the CIC, Rudolph said: "After 1930... Germany appeared to me to be headed for catastrophe. The great unemployment caused expansion of the national socialistic and communistic parties. Frightened that the [communists] would become the government, I joined the NSDAP [Nazi Party] to help, I believed, in the preservation of the Western culture."

From March 3, 1952 "Top Secret" Report of 115th CIC (Counter Intelligence Corps), U.S. Army headed "Schreiber, Walter Paul (Paperclip)":

"1.... Dr. Schreiber indicated satisfaction with [U.S.] provisions being made pending his resettlement in Argentina. Schreiber professed rabid anti-communist feelings and promised denial [of U.S. resettlement of him] of any interviews with press [before leaving United States]."

Dr. Schreiber was a Project Paperclip scientist found guilty of carrying out experiments on prisoners at Dachau and Auschwitz, 1941-1943. He helped direct B-W (Bacteriological Warfare) program of U.S. Air Force, 1948-1951. The above "Top Secret" exchange between the CIC and U.S. Air Force Intelligence (A-2) shows how these authorities arranged for his escape ("resettlement") to Argentina after the Air Force was forced to drop Schreiber from its payroll. A careful reading of subsequent intelligence telexes indicates that Schreiber in fact "resettled" in Paraguay in 1952.

Excerpted from "U.S. Passport for Genocide,"
by Charles R. Allen, Jr., *Keeping Posted,* October 1980

Former CIA Chief Defends Use of Charged Nazi War Criminals

On the day the Rudolph story broke, Ted Koppel's ABC "Nightline News" network program elicited from Ray S. Cline, for 23 years Deputy Director of Intelligence for the Central Intelligence Agency (CIA), a vigorous defense of his organization's utilization of Dr. Rudolph and other charged Nazi war criminals.

The erstwhile CIA chief's unabashed apologies for Rudolph triggered strong reactions throughout the media and the more than 40 million viewers of "Nightline."

The *Jewish Telegraphic Agency* (JTA) characterized Cline's commentary as "a blatant apologia for the utilization of Nazi war criminals" and a TV critic scored the former number two man at CIA for his "insufferable arrogance."

Host Ted Koppel had asked Cline: "Should [Rudolph] have been forced to go back to [West] Germany or should he have been left alone?"

Cline replied: "He should have been recognized as having paid whatever debt to society his WWII activities deserved because of his [scientific and technological contribution] to the U.S. and to the strategic defenses of this country."

Notwithstanding Rudolph's guilt in the deaths of five, ten or 20 thousand people, "whatever it was he did," Mr. Koppel asked.

Cline: "... the moral issue of his particular behaviour... should not be allowed to offset this enormous benefit which we deliberately sought and got from him. I feel a little sad to see him now deprived of his American citizenship and made to feel a criminal as an old man after all these years of trying to redeem a record which many Germans have tried to redeem."

Reported JTA (October 23, 1984 by a special correspondent, Rochelle Saidel): "Nazi war criminal expert, Charles R. Allen, Jr., attacked Cline's... defense of Rudolph as a clear CIA statement justifying utilization of Nazi genocidists by U.S. intelligence."

Allen stated: "That's a classic statement of CIA utilization of not only Rudolph but others [war criminals] which has been proven by myself and other journalists in quite a few instances."

JTA reported further: "Cline attempted to shore up his defense of Rudolph by bringing up the name of [General] Reinhard Gehlen, chief of Nazi intelligence on the Russian Front who later ran the CIA's anti-Soviet espionage/sabotage operations in Europe" under the so-called Gehlen Org.

Cline called Gehlen a friend whom he "knew well" and who — like Rudolph —"wanted to make retribution for whatever crimes they'd committed and contribute to the welfare and security of the U.S.... That's a legitimate objective by [sic] the U.S. government to take advantage."

Allen broke in: "Gehlen of course was not an anti-Nazi, nor did he ever lead any plot to kill Hitler. He was an unreconstructed Nazi.... it was his files of operations behind the lines of the Soviet Union that the CIA used and employed, incidentally, some of the same brutalities used [during the Holocaust] by Gehlen and his [Nazi] forces..."

Cline: "That's just!...that [sic] such an obvious anti-CIA attitude. I really don't want to try to refute it. But it isn't true. I knew Gehlen well. I know the facts...I don't think you do."

Allen: "Well, I do know the facts, and I don't care how *well* you knew him personally. His objective role is very clear in history."

Mr. Koppel then questioned Cline about the CIA handbook advising Nicaraguan Contras to commit political assassinations, kidnapping and the like. The "Nightline" host wondered if there was some kind of a relationship to the use of accused Nazi war criminals. "Are we playing games here?" asked Mr. Koppel. "I mean, we seem to become morally outraged...whenever it suits our purposes."

Cline denied the thrust of the Koppel remarks. "Well, Ted, we do overdo the pure morality from time to time...This outrage over this little pamphlet is to me preposterous....It clearly isn't a CIA-type...document."

As reported by JTA:

"Allen again faced Cline down, pointing out that the first counter-insurgency training at Fort Meade, Md. (1950's) was derived from the anti-Partisan Nazi experience....[that] there was proven utilization of accused Nazi war criminals for counter-insurgency training."

Said Allen on "Nightline": "...what Mr. Cline has just asserted is very misleading...there is a direct, concrete continuum relationship between that early period of the '50's when such war criminals and collaborators were [so] used...and the CIA Nicaraguan pamphlet..."

Just seven weeks after the "Nightline" program, the Anti-Defamation League (ADL) announced its December 7th symposium on "international terrorism."

The ADL's headliner: Ray S. Cline, former number two CIA director. In response to inquiries by the JTA, the ADL defended its use of Cline who was characterized by JTA as "a blatant CIA apologist in behalf of used Nazi war criminals."

Former Congresswoman Elizabeth Holtzman and Brooklyn (N.Y.) District Attorney told JTA: "I think it's wrong for the Jewish community to give a platform to a person who condones the murders of Arthur Rudolph."

Abraham Foxman, ADL's director of international affairs who organized the symposium, said: "Cline's comments on 'Nightline' do not make him a *personna non grata*...His [Cline's] expertise on terrorism is in tune with what we [ADL] believe in."

Reported the JTA: "Cline was also the featured speaker at the World Anti-Communist League (WACL) convention September 3-7 in San Diego, Calif. Charles Allen Jr. described WACL to the JTA as '[a] major international fascist organization at the highest levels.' Past speakers have included well-known racists, anti-Semites and fascists such as Theodor Oberlander, the notorious SS commander and accused Nazi war criminal."

Other Paperclip Nazis

Two Paperclip specialists figured tangentially in the 1984 Rudolph story. Essential data and relevance are noted briefly below.

- **Rickhey, Dr. Georg** — was director general of Dora-Nordhausen slave labor/rocket factory 1943-1945. As such on all Allied wanted war criminals lists. Came to United States under Project Paperclip in 1945 as expert on "Guided Missiles." Was returned to stand trial as defendant during 1947 Dora war crimes trial. Was Rudolph's superior at Dora. Rickhey was acquitted. Despite trial and substantial evidence of his complicity, Rickhey was listed as one of "the German specialists...in whom U.S. military agencies have a continuing interest" (Joint Intelligence Objective Agency — JIOA of Project Paperclip — Restricted Memorandum, as of 1 June 1948, Objective List, Revision II, Preface). Besides Rickhey's name was comment: "On Trial for War Crimes." Rickhey was a member of the Nazi Party. After trial, Rickhey reportedly employed by re-established military industry in West Germany and in its missile programs.

- **Ehricke, Dr. Krafft A.F.** — German rocket/missile scientist, born, Berlin, March 24, 1917, educated Berlin University in celestial mechanics, studied under the famous physicist, Werner Heisenberg. Was engineer in Nazi V-rockets program, finished career at the Dora-

Nordhausen slave labor/rocket factory complex. Came to U.S. 1947, worked in Werner von Braun's "German rocket team" until 1952 when he entered military-industrial corporations. Worked at Bell Aircraft in Buffalo, N.Y. under Major General Walter Dornberger, himself an accused Nazi war criminal for his activities as chief executive officer of the Dora-Nordhausen complex. (Dornberger was also a Paperclip alumnus who served as a director of several U.S. aircraft corporations and was a CIA consultant, according to information developed and published by Charles R. Allen, Jr. Dornberger died in Buffalo in the late 1970's.)

Other aerospace firms for which Ehricke worked included General Dynamics, Rockwell International Corp. and Space Global. Ehricke played a major role in the development of the powerful rockets, Atlas and Centaur used for outer space flight.

He was the recipient of numerous awards by NASA. On May 3, 1984, Ehricke received the prestigious Goddard Astronautics Award from the American Institute of Aeronautics and Astronautics.

Not widely known is the fact of Ehricke's membership in the Fusion Energy Foundation (FEF) and his listing on the editorial advisory board of FEF's official magazine, *Fusion*. The May-June 1984 issue of *Fusion* carried an article by Ehricke on colonizing the moon.

The Fusion Energy Foundation is a well-known front group of the Lyndon H. LaRouche pro-fascist, anti-Semitic National Caucus of Labor Committees (NCLC) — a curious, turgid and mysteriously financed operation. *Fusion* promotes nuclear energy plants and various concoctions of 'Star Wars' weaponry, including "beam" weaponry.

According to a special issue of *The New Republic* (November 19, 1984), the LaRouchian "leaders of a lunatic movement have conferred repeatedly with top [Reagan] Administration officials" and the CIA.

LaRouchian liaisons with the CIA are a matter of record.

According to several well-documented studies, the LaRouche-led groups have intimate alliances with the KKK, the largest anti-Semitic group in the United States, Liberty Lobby, and para-military, neo-Nazi organizations in Western Europe and Latin America.

Whatever the precise extent of the relationship between LaRouche's FEF and *Fusion* magazine on the one hand and Ehricke on the other, it remains the first demonstrated nexus between the American Far Right and the Paperclip scientists of Nazi Germany. Further in-depth investigations are required of this vital development.

On December 11, 1984 at his home in La Jolla, Calif., Krafft Ehricke died. He was 67 years old. *The New York Times* obituary of December 13th noted that he was a scientist who had "looked beyond the engineering drawing boards to imagine bold ventures in space travel years before the first satellites were launched into orbit."

Dr. Wernher Frhr. von Braun, born March 23, 1912, Wirsitz, Germany. NSDAP #185068. SS #5738692. Promoted SS *Sturmbannfuehrer* (Major), June 28, 1943. Source: Berlin Document Center, List of SS-Officers.

Deportations:
When? How Many? ... To Where?

The 1980's witnessed the first of the final orders for deportation of individuals proven under American law to have concealed their participation in the persecutions of Nazi Germany. Based on the civil procedures initiated by an aroused Congress in the 1970's, the balance of this decade will be given over to more such deportations.

When? In 1983-1984, six persons permanently departed the United States: Lipschis to West Germany, Hrusitzky to Venezuela, Trifa to Portugal, Rudolph to West Germany, Avdzej to West Germany and Fedorenko to the U.S.S.R.

How Many? Neal M. Sher, OSI director, expects "close to a dozen" final deportation orders will be handed down by the courts over the 1984-1985 period. Such well publicized cases as those of Artukovic, Demjanjuk, Laipenieks and Maikovskis may then be determined. Of the 35 on-going trials in 1984, another dozen or so will be ordered to deportation by the late 1980's. At least 24 deportations may be expected in the 1980's.

What is the procedure? Under the law, after having exhausted all appeal routes, the charged Nazi may be deported "to a country of his/her designation." If the preferred country refuses to accept the petitioning Nazi then he has various legal options by which he can delay his departure even though a final order for deportation has been issued.

In theory, a deportable Nazi has but one preference. In practice, he can — and does — shop around for a country willing to take him. (Trifa, for example, applied for entry first to Switzerland and then four other countries over the course of nearly two years following the court's order to deportation. He finally gained a 90-day visitor's visa on August 13, 1984 to Portugal. See Trifa under *Cases No Longer Active*.)

Moreover, the Attorney General of the United States may similarly bar a Nazi's deportation to a country — even though that country may want him for war crimes or may have filed an extradition request for him — because the U.S. "believes" that "the alien would be subject to persecution on account of race, religion or political opinion."

Such determinations by the executive courts have effectively allowed the charged mass murderer, Andrija Artukovic of Yugoslavia, to stay in the United States for over 36 years.

Even though the U.S. Supreme Court ruled that Artukovic was extraditable to Yugoslavia, the country where he allegedly committed his crimes as a leader of the Ustashi terrorists, his case illustrates the central problem of the deportation process now that its ultimate consequences are at hand.

Yugoslavia is a communist nation. The United States is loathe to send even a proven and wanted Nazi war criminal to a communist nation.

It is conceivable that a proven Nazi war criminal, even after being ordered to deportation, would be permitted to remain here in a stateless condition (he could not vote or hold property, otherwise his life would not materially change).

In a 1982 Op-Ed article written for the Hearst newspapers, Charles R. Allen, Jr. pointed out: "One may well ask under such circumstances if there is life after a final deportation order for a criminal of the Holocaust in post-Nuremberg America."

Thus far, the six Nazis who have been expelled — to West Germany, Venezuela, Portugal and the U.S.S.R. — will not likely face prosecution. If Israel's extradition request for Demjanjuk of Treblinka is granted, then perhaps there may be a war crimes trial held for him.

Yet the question remains: will the several accused war criminals who have been tried and found guilty *in absentia* in the Soviet Union — such as Laipenieks, Linnas, Maikovskis, Palciauskas, Sokolov-Samarin — be deported to the U.S.S.R. where they would go to certain judgment?

Should they be so deported?

The Nuremberg Precedents

What precedents are there for the deportations of individuals found to have participated in the persecutions of Nazi Germany?

They are to be found in public statements, agreements and proclamations which the U.S. itself initiated (sometimes actually authoring the very language) during and after World War II.

First and foremost was the Moscow Declaration of 1943 when the Grand Alliance promised: "Most assuredly the Allied Powers will pursue them [Nazi war criminals and collaborators] to the uttermost ends of the earth and deliver them to their accusers in order that justice may be done."

Other agreements and procedures for the return of such ilk *"to their accusers"* were worked out at the Nuremberg Tribunals (1945-1949) based on the 1945 London Agreement which was the statutory authority for those trials held collectively and individually by all members of the Grand Alliance.

These novel legal principles and precepts were then broadened during the course of the immediate postwar years to include crimes against humanity; namely, "murder, extermination, enslavement, deportation and other inhumane acts... against any civilian population... or persecutions on political, racial or religious grounds."

(It should be noted that every accused Nazi found guilty under the OSI proceedings has been judged to have participated in such crimes.)

Much of the world community has, since Nuremberg, kneaded these precedents into their own national *corpus juris.*

Not a single nation which was a party to these wartime compacts has repudiated them. Indeed, the U.S. State Department specifically reaffirmed the validity of the 1945 London Agreement as recently as 1982 when questions were raised by Charles R. Allen, Jr. in a series of Op-Ed articles subsequently published internationally.

Various resolutions of the United Nations have extended these compacts. In 1947, the U.N. General Assembly unanimously affirmed that "members of the U.N. [will] take all necessary measures to cause them [wanted Nazi war criminals] to be sent back to the countries in which their abominable deeds were done in order that they may be judged and punished according to the laws of these countries."

Professor John H.E. Fried, internationally renowned scholar on war crimes and criminality who was Special Consultant to the U.S. War Crimes Tribunals at Nuremberg (1947-1949), told an international conference held in Albany, N.Y., April 27th-29th, 1984 that every party to the Nuremberg agreements in the aggregate are required by international law *"to hand over"* a wanted Nazi war criminal to any "concerned" nation that was a victim of Nazi war crimes.

In this respect, Israel in 1983 requested the extradition of Demjanjuk who has been ordered to deportation (see *Deportation Cases*). Israel did not exist during World War II but is considered a properly "concerned" nation, in large part, founded as a haven for the victims of Hitler's Final Solution. Members of the Grand Alliance have *prima facie* status when requesting that accused Nazi criminals be "handed over."

The Oct. 30, 1978 Holtzman Law (so-called after its author, then Congresswoman Elizabeth Holtzman, D-N.Y.) reinforces what is called "the Nuremberg processes" vis-a-vis Nazi war criminals.

Further elucidating on this precise point, Robert A. Cohen, Esq., wrote in *The Journal of International Law and Politics* about American legal responsibilities toward such "coextensive international agreements" as the 1943 Moscow Declaration: "The United States committed itself to bringing to judgment those persons who had [perpetrated] atrocities — either by returning them to the areas where they committed their heinous crimes or by delivering them to the International Tribunal for trial. . . ."

According to this legal expert, "The [Holtzman Act] conforms with this moral commitment made by the United States."

Writing further on the Op-Ed pages of scores of American newspapers, Charles R. Allen, Jr. reported and commented in late 1982 as follows:

"There is talk in Washington that clearly precludes the deportation of any Nazi war criminal, so found in our own courts after all due process and appeals have been properly exhausted by the defendant, to a communist nation where, in fact, he perpetrated crimes during the Final Solution and may be wanted for those crimes.

"Such predeterminations palpably are contrary to the legal precedents established at Nuremberg as well as the moral spirit of that international monument.

"Moreover, such arbitrary debarment would also shortcircuit the truly historic achievements which our own legal system is crafting by way of the OSI trials which have already garnered landmark decisions before the U.S. Supreme Court [Fedorenko] and the U.S. Courts of Appeals [Linnas, Palciauskas] and the Board of Immigration Appeals of the INS [Laipenieks].

"In those cases, our own courts have considered and duely held that our juridical conduct in the OSI Nazi cases are consistent with both our own law and international law. There will likely be further rulings [Allen wrote] affecting not only our own immigration law but the greater body of law vis-a-vis the Nuremberg system itself.

"This sense of a civilized process must be permitted to make its way to an unequivocal resolution; most especially at its final stage, namely, deportation. This process is concerned with justice, not vengeance. Therefore, let it inexorably go forward to *its final resolution.*

"Proven Nazi war criminals found in our midst, and prosecuted in our own courts must, therefore, not merely be expelled from our shores but deported to stand trial at last on the soil where they shed innocent blood.

"This is the law, the international law," Allen concluded.

Such apprehensions as articulated in the 1982-1984 Allen Op-Ed series were further reinforced by a Special Report issued by The Hon. Peter W. Rodino, Jr., chairman of the Judiciary Committee of the U.S. House of

Representatives, one of the most powerful standing committees of the U.S. Congress. On May 15, 1984, he stated:

- "Despite the excellent work of OSI, the Judiciary Committee remains *deeply concerned about the efforts of the Department of State* to assist the Justice Department and OSI in arranging the deportation of war criminals ordered to leave the United States. Although at the request of OSI, *the State Department has made routine inquiries* to foreign governments about accepting these individuals, *it seems unwilling to pursue this subject aggressively.*

"Much of the burden, therefore, has fallen to OSI to locate countries where these criminals can be sent. *This must not continue to be the case.*

"Only with the State Department's active and strenuous participation will those foreign governments with a moral or legal obligation to accept war criminals understand that the United States is fully committed to this effort and expects cooperation from other nations. *The State Department's apparent failure to recognize this fact seriously undermines the work of OSI and tarnishes its victories in court"* (Report 98-759, 98th Congress, 2nd Session, p. 7, emphases added).

A senior official of the World Jewish Congress (WJC) then charged that the State Department "was engaged in a deliberate and callous policy of sabotaging efforts to deport convicted Nazi war criminals from this country."

Kalman Sultanik of the WJC cited the Rodino report as confirmation of his accusation. "When the actions of one governmental agency — in this case the State Department — seeks to undermine the work of another agency — the Justice Department — the American people have a right to an explanation," said Dr. Sultanik. (*The Baltimore Jewish Times,* July 20, 1984, dispatch of *Jewish Telegraphic Agency.*)

Scoring the 1984 deportation of Archbishop Trifa as a "travesty" that has "allowed [this] abettor of genocide to fly into retirement to the sunny beaches of Portugal," Charles R. Allen, Jr. wrote on the prestigious editorial pages of *The Boston Globe* (August 30, 1984): "Is this what we are to expect — and *accept* — with the dozen or so cases of deportation orders that will become final over the ensuing year for the genocidists among us?"

Headlined *The Globe*: "A lesson in duplicity as U.S. lets Nazi war criminal avoid justice."

In Portugal itself, second thoughts were evident as one of the country's largest weeklies, *O'Jornal,* featured the comments of Allen, former OSI prosecutor Eli M. Rosenbaum and others. Talk in Lisbon grew that Trifa would be the object of demands for his expulsion by the Portugese government.

Already, the Trifa deportation suggests persuasively that this final aspect of the entire issue of Nazi war criminals in the United States remains ambiguous and, therefore, unresolved.

State Department "Not Aggressive" on Nazi Deportations, says Congress

"For the seventh consecutive year, the Judiciary Committee has specifically earmarked funds ($3.3 million fiscal 1985)... for the Office of Special Investigations (OSI)... which is responsible for investigating and prosecuting denaturalization and deportation actions against alleged Nazi war criminals living in the United States.

"Despite the excellent work of OSI, the Judiciary Committee remains deeply concerned about the efforts of the Department of State to assist the Justice Department and OSI in arranging the deportation of war criminals ordered to leave the United States. Although, at the request of OSI, the State Department has made routine inquiries to foreign governments about accepting these individuals, it seems unwilling to pursue the subject aggressively. Much of the burden, therefore, has fallen to OSI to locate countries where these criminals can be sent. This must not continue to be the case. Only with the State Department's active and strenuous participation will those foreign governments with a moral or legal obligation to accept war criminals understand that the U.S. is fully committed to this effort and expects cooperation from other nations. The State Department's apparent failure to recognize this fact seriously undermines the work of OSI and tarnishes its victories in court."

U.S. Congressman Peter W. Rodino, Jr.
(D-N.J.), Chairman, Judiciary Committee,
U.S. House of Representatives
(Report 98-759), May 15, 1984

DENATURALIZATION CASES

Case	#	Won	Lost	Originated INS	Originated OSI	Status On Appeal	Status Unresolved+
Artishenko, B. ‡	×				×		×
Gudauskas, V.	×				×		×
Juodis, J.	×				×		×
Kairys, L.	×				×		×
Klimavicius, J.	×				×		×
Kowalchuk, S.	×		×	×		×	
Koziy, B.	×	×			×		×
Kungys, J.	×		×		×	×	×
Palciauskas, K.	×	×			×		×
Schuk, M.	×				×		×
Sokolov (Samarin), V.	×				×		×
Sprogis, E.	×		×		×	×	×
Virkutis, A.	×				×		×
TOTALS:	13	2	3	1	12	3	12

Denaturalization Cases

Unresolved+   In denaturalization cases, an "unresolved" matter means: if not on appeal then waiting possible filing of appeal from trial judge's decision; or that because of physical or mental difficulties, the defendant is no longer able to stand trial but is subject to periodic examination before a final determination is made; or, in certain instances, the U.S. Government is faced with a probable loss on appeal. It should be bourne in mind that a win for the Government at a denaturalization trial means that deportation hearings before a Board of Immigration judge follow. That step may be appealed at the next step, the Board of Immigration Appeals (BIA). The Government may appeal an adverse BIA decision by appealing to the U.S. Solicitor General.

Of the grand total of 31 unresolved cases at trial, 6 at the denaturalization courts are ongoing and no decision has yet been handed down; additionally, 2 others have not been acted upon by OSI after two years since the decision.

There are 16 unresolved deportation trials of which the OSI has prevailed in 9; the next step of the long appeal process available to the defense will no doubt be taken. This too prolongs the "unresolved" nature of these trials.

Within both the Deportation and Cases "No Longer Active" categories, there have been some cases — notably Hazners, Detlavs and Soobzokov — that, regardless of OSI explanations, have been irrevocably lost. Of the several others in this amorphous area, there has been a curious absence of vigorous follow-ups by the OSI.

Of the 31 "unresolved" cases, therefore, less than half are considered so because of the legal processes; slightly more than half are in limbo.

(‡ See page 67.)

DEPORTATION CASES

Case	#	Won	Lost	Originated INS	Originated OSI	Status On Appeal	Status Unresolved+
Artukovic, A.	×			×		×	×
Benkunskas, H.	×				×		×
Bernotas, A.	×				×		×
Demjanjuk, J.	×	×		×			×
Hazners, V.	×		×	×			×
Kaminskas, B.	×			×			×
Kisilaitis, J.	×				×		×
Kulle, A.	×				×	×	×
Laipenieks, E.	×		×		×	×	×
Lehmann, A.	×	×			×		×
Linnas, K.	×	×			×		×
Maikovskis, B.	×	×		×			×
Paskevicius, M.	×	×			×		×
Schellong, C.	×	×			×		×
Theodorovich, G.	×	×			×		×
TOTALS:	**15**	**7**	**2**	**5**	**10**	**3**	**15**

Deportation Cases

Unresolved+ Most cases herein have been filed too recently for a decision by trial judge, hence these trials, having just commenced, have not reached any decision. In certain cases — such as that of Vilis Hazners, the Latvian Waffen SS officer — the U.S. Government has been "considering various possible courses of action"; in Hazners, OSI, since losing its appeal on July 15, 1981, has continued to repeat this fiction. Hence that case may be termed technically as "unresolved," for practical purposes it has clearly been lost. Cases lost by the defendants at trial are thus marked indicating they have the option to appeal their setbacks before the BIA.

CASES "NO LONGER ACTIVE"*

Case	#	Won	Lost	No Action By OSI	Status Deported	Death	Illness	Originated INS	OSI
Avdzej, J. ‡	×	×			×				×
von Bolschwing, O.	×	×				×			×
Dercacz, M.	×	×				×			×
Detlavs, K.	×		×			×	×		
Deutscher, A.	×					×			×
Fedorenko, F. ‡	×	×			×		×		
Hrusitzky, A. ‡	×	×			×				×
Karklins, T.	×					×			×
Kowalchuk, M.	×			×			×		
Lipschis, HJ. ‡	×	×			×				×
Osidach, W.	×	×				×			×
Popczuk, M.	×					×			×
Rudolph, A. ‡	×	×			×				×
Soobzokov, T.	×		×	×					×
Trifa, V. ‡	×	×			×			×	
Trucis, A.	×					×			×
Walus, F.	×		×	×				×	
TOTALS:	17	9	3	3	6	8		5	12

Cases "No Longer Active"*

* A somewhat imprecise category used by the OSI, hence placed in quotation marks. Of the 17 cases in this category, 8 of the defendants have died, 6 have been deported and 3 have not been acted upon by the OSI. Of the 6 deportations (as of February 1, 1985), 5 absented themselves from the U.S. under an arrangement with the OSI thus precluding trial. Each is permanently barred from re-entering the U.S. Not a single one of the 6 deportation cases has been sent back to face justice on the soil on which he committed the crimes concealed when he first entered the U.S.

‡ These are clearly plea bargaining settlements. As such they utterly are violative of Nuremberg processes regarding "handing over" war criminals to primary-interest nation.

SUMMARIES
U.S. vs CHARGED NAZI WAR CRIMINALS IN USA*

Category	Totals	1977-1985 Won	Lost	Deportations	On Appeal	Unresolved	Deaths	Origin INS	OSI
Denaturalization (Ongoing)	13	2	3		3	12		1	12
Deportation (Ongoing)	15	7	2		3	15		5	10
"No Longer Active"	17	9	3	6		3	8	5	12
TOTALS TO DATE 1985:	**45**	**18**	**8**	**6**	**6**	**30**	**8**	**11**	**34**

(as of April 1985)

Some Salient Aspects

The above charts derive from the official OSI "Digest of Cases in Litigation." July 1, 1984, December 31, 1984 communication and January 1, 1985. Certain data show the following salient aspects:

• OSI has filed 34 cases over its five years in existence, three times as many as the INS filed (11) in the two years of its operation. Thus OSI has averaged approximately 6.4 cases filed a year, INS about 5.5 cases a year.

• As of this writing, there have been six actual deportations. Five originated with OSI. The first deportation under the OSI/INS legal process was in April 1983, nearly six years after this process began. (See •* p. 69.)

• Of the total number of 45 cases to date, 30 have for various reasons yet to be resolved. Eight cases have additionally been rendered moot by the deaths/suicides of the defendants. Thus for practical purposes the preponderant majority of the cases filed by the Government over seven years have not yet been ultimately determined.

• A further perplexity may be seen in the title of OSI's listings, "Digest of Cases in Litigation." According to OSI's own category of 17 cases called "No Longer Active," the title of the Digest becomes a slight misnomer; more precisely it should be "OSI Digest of Cases."

• Six deportations by 1983-1985 represent a little better than a 13% rate of success to complaints filed over a seven year period. The OSI admits to having worked up their cases for court trials from an original listing of "over

480" individual accused Nazi war criminals in the United States. This means about a 10% triability rate. (Most knowledgeable students of this issue assume the 480 figure is extremely conservative; while there likely are many more, no one will know the precise number who found haven in the United States.) In any event, the statistical results — notwithstanding the clearly talented and dedicated effort of OSI — are of little consequence. In turn, this lamentable conclusion is clearly *not* a criticism of the OSI but rather a commentary on the United States itself over the past 35 years.

●* Three deportations (Hrusitzky, Lipschis and Trifa) may be technically considered as such. Two cases (Avdzej and Rudolph) are clearly departures or arranged expulsions; but hardly clear-cut deportations. Fedorenko is an expulsion of unknown consequences. Such ambiguous cases may well prove to be precedents for what will increasingly become the *modus vivendi* for getting war criminals out of the United States. In effect, some legal sources and political observers argue, they are in fact a form of plea bargaining as applied to these unique trials. Thus one must keep such arrangements in mind when considering OSI claims about "deportations" and "victories" in court.

A Special Note

- **Artukovic, Andrija** — Ordered extradited March 4, 1985. Secretary of State George Shultz may determine final disposition by April 4, 1985.

  Two cases do not appear in the above listings and charts. They are:

- **Bogdanovs, Boleslavs** — 66-year-old Latvian, entered U.S. in 1956, naturalized 1964. Accused by OSI of mass murders in Madona, Latvia during World War II. Defendant allegedly was Latvian security policeman under SS control. Bogdanovs is now an architect for the city of Hartford, Conn. Denaturalization suit. Defendant had no comment regarding charges for AP on November 29, 1983.

- **Katin, Matthew** — This individual accused by OSI on November 9, 1984 of having served in SS-controlled Lithuanian *Schutzmannschaft*. Individual resides in Norwood, Mass., born, Lithuania, 1914, according to AP and UPI wire stories in November 1984. Pre-trial discovery as of March 1985.

Neal Sher, OSI director, did not return telephone inquiries regarding these matters. While the media have carried the sketchy details reported here, these cases will *not* be included among the official litigation breakouts of the OSI because of that office's failure to respond in timely fashion.

The Mengele Case: U.S. Involvement?

The most publicized war criminal yet at large is Dr. Josef Mengele, born March 16, 1911 in Guenzberg, Germany. SS physician at Auschwitz where he carried out medical experiments on inmates, especially twin children, in order to breed perfect Nordic specimens. Called "The Angel of Death," he was one of the SS doctors who made "selections" of arriving prisoners: *recht* (right) to slave labor at Auschwitz; *links* (left) to Birkenau and the gas chambers.

Life on the Run

Most of the published claims about Mengele's escape and subsequent life on the run is contradictory, devoid of documented proof and exploitatively sensationalistic. Thus when considering the Mengele matter, one must exercise caution.

The facts of his post-war years are sketchy. Allegedly, he spent some time in 1945 as an interned patient in a British hospital in occupied Germany. He then supposedly lived openly at his family's home in Guenzberg. The Mengele family's wealth derives from its multi-national firm that manufactures and distributes agricultural implements and heavy machinery. Reasonable assumptions are that the family has in large measure supported Mengele since the war.

When accusations against him became a public problem, Mengele dropped from sight in 1949. He allegedly used the "monastery routes" to flee Europe, exiting at Genoa with false papers under the name "Gregorio Gregori," making his way first to Franco Spain, thence to Argentina with a passport bearing his real name and photograph. (No documented evidence of this purported passage has ever been produced.)

In Argentina, Mengele supposedly practiced medicine openly in Buenos Aires and environs. On June 5, 1959, a murder warrant was issued against him by a Freiberg, West German court. Among its 17 specific accusations: "Mengele killed...a newborn baby...by throwing the infant into an open fire before the eyes of its mother."

For more than six months, the West German foreign ministry — itself notoriously packed with Nazis from Hitler's ministry of foreign affairs — did not circulate the extradition request based on the murder warrant to those countries where Mengele had been sighted.

Mengele in the meantime was shuttling among Argentina, Paraguay and Brazil, according to sources. In late October of 1959, he purportedly was naturalized in Paraguay. (Some sources say the date was 1957.) Not until

June 28, 1960 did Argentina itself assign the extradition requests for proceedings to get underway.

From the 1960's, innumerable sightings of Mengele have been carried by the world media. Often he has been "positively" identified at one and the same moment in Brazil, Argentina, Paraguay, Uruguay, Colombia, etc. Waves of "Mengelitis," as it were, have convulsed the West every five years or so.

1966 FBI Report and U.S. Nazis

A copy of a "Confidential" FBI report on "Joseph Mengele" dated December 8, 1966 and carrying an allegation by an "informant" that "the wanted Nazi war criminal JOSEPH MENGELE is masquerading under the name of HAROLD ENDINAN and resides in Riviera, Arizona" has been circulating among self-described U.S. "Nazi hunters" for years.

(The author of *The Basic Handbook* was once asked to join a West Coast radio program to "expose" this "latest development"; the invitation was declined.)

The FBI report carried a note that read: "The files of the Los Angeles Office [of the FBI] reflect that [deletion] aka [also known as] Joseph Mengele, was the subject of a report of SA [Special Agent] [deletion] dated 2/9/44 at New York, N.Y. He was the subject of Denaturalization Proceedings apparently because his name appeared on Nazi Party list."

The author of *The Basic Handbook* has in his research library the complete report of the U.S. Senate Committee on Military Affairs issued in August 1946, titled "Nazi Party Membership Records." (79th Congress, 2d Session) in which appears the names of 680 American citizens who were secret members of the AO (*Auslandsorganisation* or Overseas Sections) of the *Nationalsocialistische Deutsche Arbeiter Partei* or Nazi Party of the Third Reich.

On page 9 of that report, there appears the name of "Mengele, Josef" whose Nazi Party "Membership Number" was 05735 (a very early enlistment) who entered the United States on August 1, 1932 and who was born in Munich on January 1, 1904. This Mengele lived at 2256 Haviland Ave. in the Bronx, N.Y. and his occupation was that of a "warehouseman."

It is not known whether an FBI follow-up on the list of American members of the German Nazi Party was ever undertaken. Since 1972, no investigations by the Justice Department's several prosecutory units were carried out.

A typical example of media exploitation was a screaming front page of the *New York Post* which hit the streets of the nation's largest city as recently as October 1, 1984: "'Angel of Death' Nazi May Be Living in Florida!!!" Its flaming "Extra!" featured the demand of an Israeli "Nazi hunter" that his "new evidence" obliged "Pres. Reagan have U.S. authorities arrest Mengele who may be living in retirement in Florida."

Among the few sober documents was an October 1973 report by Poland's war crimes commission alleging that Mengele was living in Amambay provence in Paraguay along the Brazilian border. Paraguay of course has been a notorious haven for Nazis since World War II. More than half of the country's economy is controlled by German interests. Its army was trained successively by Imperial and Nazi militarists since World War I. Its dictator, General Alfredo Stroessner, an open admirer of Hitler, controls one of Latin America's most oppressive regimes. Stroessner has rebuffed all attempts to flush out Mengele, let alone honor any legal steps seeking extradition.

U.S. Army Documents on Mengele

Writing in *The New York Times* of January 23, 1985, Ralph Blumenthal described 14 documents declassified and released in December 1984 by the U.S. Army Intelligence and Security Command's FOI (Freedom of Information) Office.

The documents had been provided to the Simon Wiesenthal Center, Los Angeles, Calif. in response to an FOI request concerning Mengele. Two of them were noted — with qualification — by Mr. Blumenthal.

The CIC in U.S.-Occupied Germany, reported *The Times,* "had received information that Dr. Mengele 'has been arrested in Vienna.'"

"An informant," continued *The Times,* "'stated that to the best of his knowledge Dr. Mengele was arrested in the U.S. Zone of Germany' — an apparently erroneous reference to Vienna where the 430th (CIC) unit was stationed."

If the report were true, 430th CIC in Vienna should have interrogated Mengele regarding the fate of "20 Jewish children removed by [Mengele] from Auschwitz in November 1944."

On January 30, *The Times* interviewed the officer who had sent the 1947 letter to Vienna. Today a resident of Israel where he had emigrated in 1949, the former CIC agent told the newspaper that "he had never heard back" from the Vienna-based CIC.

A careful reading of the 1947 CIC letter suggests that Mengele — who was described as "one Dr. Mengele, fnu [first name unknown, CRA] former [chief medical officer] in Auschwitz Extermination Camp" — may very well have been arrested in the U.S. Zone.

The sender of the letter to the Vienna CIC went on to say: "Consequently, if this information is correct, your office should be informed of the arrest and the present whereabouts of the Subject [Mengele]."

The question arises: why would a CIC agent in U.S.-Occupied Germany be informing Vienna of an arrest it has already made and of Mengele's present whereabouts which, presumably, is with the Vienna CIC?

Paragraph 3 has equally confusing language: "*Subject [Mengele] can be located* and if an interrogation of Subject by CIC or upon request of the CIC is possible" then Mengele should be questioned about the missing children from Auschwitz.

The Times deduced that an "apparent erroneous reference" had been made by the CIC from the Vth Region in Bavaria in regard to the arrest of Mengele in U.S.-Occupied Germany.

Perhaps another shading of the 1947 CIC inquiry is that Mengele may well have been arrested earlier in the U.S. Zone of Germany and subsequently arrested again in Vienna. Both points are speculative from which surmisals are made at risk.

Clearly, the primary concern of the 1947 CIC letter is not Mengele but rather the fate of the 20 children some of whose surviving parents, stated the letter, were "most eager to have news...about their children."

That the CIC agent who sent the 1947 missive did not know the first name of Mengele and apparently knew little about Mengele's background reinforces this observation.

The several 3x5 "Identification" and "Master Cards" carrying brief notes on Mengele can not be exactly dated nor are they$_0$ referenced as accompanying enclosures.

(Moreover, the press handouts of the Wiesenthal group are reduced and unreadable, prompting complaints from the media that covered the 1985 press conference. This writer received the fully released Mengele files in their original, more readable state.)

Regardless of the questions and vagueness surrounding the April 26, 1947 document; and, notwithstanding the possibility of Mengele having been arrested not once but twice, the question remains unanswered: did the CIC ever realize whom they had arrested?

The Canadian Connection

The second document of importance — dated June 26, 1962 — was executed when Mengele's crimes were well-known and documented. There could be no excuse whatsoever for not knowing who he was.

An intelligence officer of the U.S. Army in Europe responded to a query from a Canadian visa control officer with offices in the Canadian Embassy in Cologne, West Germany.

Reported *The Times*: "This letter (June 26, 1962) is a response to a query concerning a 'Joseph Menke' who," *The Times* qualified, "evidently had applied for a Canadian visa in Buenos Aires."

The attachment from the American intelligence officer to the Canadian visa control officer was a one page, three paragraph form providing a physical description of Mengele, incorrectly giving him the rank of an *Obersturmfuehrer* (First Lieutenant) at Auschwitz (he had left Auschwitz as a *Hauptsturmfuehrer* or Captain of the SS) and further describing Mengele as "the notorious camp surgeon at Auschwitz" still at large and wanted by West German authorities for the large Auschwitz trials scheduled for Frankfort late 1962.

Nowhere among the pages released to the Wiesenthal group is there any evidence of precisely what the Canadian inquiry had specified. There is the *assumption* here that "Menke" (who was *not* known to the U.S. intelligence officer responding to the Canadian) is Mengele. There is not a single concrete fact for such an assumption. Consider the following:

• The U.S. Army's Intelligence and Security Command FOI (Freedom of Information) Office December 5, 1984 responded to Rabbi Marvin Hier of the Wiesenthal Center that "a search was made... using the various aliases of Josef Mengele provided" by Hier. "As a result of this search we were unable to locate any records under the aliases," the Army stated.

• The Army Intelligence FOI Office located and released 14 declassified pages through the names "Josef Megele" and "Bernhard Mosberg" (the latter was the name of one of Mengele's victims which has no bearing on the hunt for Mengele.) *These pages were unearthed solely by the Army FOI unit, not from Hier's leads.*

• A 3x5 card headed "X Menke, Joseph" carries a sub-notation, "See Mengele, Joseph for other names used," lists 19 May 1911 as "Menke's" birthdate (Mengele's usual birth date is March 16, 1911), shows his occupation as doctor and his residence as Argentina. Is this a Canadian document? Probably not as an American agency can not release a Canadian government document without the latter's permission. *There is nothing on this 3x5 (bearing an indistinguishable date) to firmly show that "Menke" applied for a Canadian visa from Buenos Aires.*

Yet the Wiesenthal Center in a handout dated January 23, 1985, asserts flatly that "the man Joseph Menke, who was seeking a Canadian visa, was in fact Josef Mengele." If such was the conclusion of U.S. Intelligence, the Wiesenthal group rhetorically asked, "Why did they not inform the Federal Republic of Germany, where Mengele was wanted for crimes against humanity, that Menke (Mengele) had applied for a Canadian visa in Buenos Aires?"

Furthermore, claimed the Wiesenthal organization, "Menke's (Josef Mengele) application [for a visa] is believed to have been made in Buenos Aires in late May or early June 1962, requesting entrance to Canada as a landed immigrant."

Hier, described as the Dean of the Center which "bears the mandate of Simon Wiesenthal," told *The New York Times* (Jan. 23, 1985) that the CIC documents "create reasonable doubt as to whether or not the U.S. had a role in the case of Josef Mengele." Hier was not specific as to what role he was alluding to; he called for an "official investigation" by both Canada and the United States.

Canada: No Mengele

On February 19, 1985, a *Jewish Telegraphic Agency* (JTA) story filed out of Toronto reported that "Recently released documents by U.S. Sen. Alfonse D'Amato (R.-NY) and the Royal Canadian Mounted Police (RCMP) indicate that Josef Mengele did not apply to come to Canada and was never in this country [Canada], contrary to allegations made last month [January 23rd] by the Simon Wiesenthal Center's Canadian representative, Sol Littman."

Littman, the JTA dispatch continued, had "dropped a bombshell" at a Canadian press conference held simultaneously with the New York release.

"Mengele had applied for the [visa] papers at Canada's embassy in Buenos Aires in 1962," the JTA said. "Littman said Mengele used the alias Joseph Menke, and that security checks showed he was really Mengele."

The JTA story went on: "However, Littman had only the U.S. side of the correspondence between Canada and the U.S. on this matter. The Canadian side was not released until February 15th because Washington needed permission from Canada to do so. . . . The complete correspondence makes it clear that Mengele never came to Canada."

The JTA also reported that a "man who was living in southern Ontario and using the name Joseph Menke was not Mengele."

The author of *The Basic Handbook* interviewed Sol Littman, a Canadian author and free-lance lecturer who wrote a 1983 book titled *War Criminal on Trial* about a Ukrainian, Helmut Rauca, who was extradited to face war crimes charges in West Germany.

When I asked him on February 22nd by telephone if the JTA filing of February 19th was accurate, Mr. Littman affirmed "yes, that's about right though I do not recall talking with a JTA correspondent."

Mr. Littman explained that the Canadian government had released one of the four documents which had been denied the Wiesenthal Center by the U.S. Army's FOI Office because they "concerned foreign government information."

The Canadian government's release of the document in question prompted Mr. Littman to call a hurriedly called press conference on February 19th where he disavowed the Wiesenthal group's previous claims.

The released document is dated June 18, 1962 and signed by Glen M. Bailey, RCMP (Royal Canadian Mounted Police) security officer in charge of monitoring visa applications at the Canadian Embassy in Cologne, West Germany, the recipient of the June 26th letter from the U.S. Intelligence officer regarding "Menke."

Bailey had asked for information concerning Mengele. He did not make any claims that Menke was Mengele. He stressed such records as fingerprints, birth certificates and asked the American to expedite his information.

I asked if the Canadian missive of June 18, 1962 was the basis for concluding that Mengele had not applied for a visa and did not come to Canada. I further questioned what "concrete linkage" in "source documentation" was there in the American-Canadian exchange that would warrant the conclusion that Menke was Mengele.

Mr. Littman explained that "my Canadian intelligence sources, former senior intelligence officers, and Canadian immigration sources" concluded that neither had the visa officer nor the American intelligence officer in any way agreed that Menke was Mengele, so the matter was dropped.

Why then had not his "intelligence sources and advisers" exercised the same caution in the absence of any concrete linkage from the American side?

Mr. Littman said, "These two documents (June 18 and June 26, 1962) indicate the nature of a routine inquiry and since there was nothing of substance that took place, we've concluded: One, Menke did *not* apply to come to Canada. Two, he did in fact not come here. And three, the Menke reported to be living in southern Ontario, an old, old rumor, is not Mengele because the Canadian Royal Mounted Police had checked him out."

"This clearly indicates your (Wiesenthal) Center's assertions then are entirely wrong, does it not?" I asked.

Mr. Littman replied, "Well, no. Just in this instance."

Further attempts to probe deeper into this curious development were turned aside by Mr. Littman.

When told that Senator D'Amato had given an "exclusive" to the weekly Orthodox newspaper in New York, *The Jewish Press* (Feb. 22, 1985) and *The Jewish Week of New York* about the release of the Canadian document on February 15th, Mr. Littman, a normally calm person, became somewhat agitated.

"Well, if he did, he didn't let me know about it!"

I then read an editorial claim by *Jewish Press* accompanying its D'Amato "exclusive": "This week some of that [Canadian] information was released and suggests that the man the Canadians were suspect of might very well have been the notorious Dr. Mengele."

Mr. Littman quickly terminated the interview.

The one-page document released to Senator D'Amato with the consent of the Canadian government on February 8, 1985 is a letter dated June 18, 1962. The Canadian visa control officer at the embassy in Cologne, West Germany made an inquiry of U.S. intelligence regarding uncorroborated "information [about a man] residing in Canada using the name of Joseph Menke may be identical to Joseph Mengele."

The Canadians asked for any "verified information" on Mengele, his wife and his son, including photographs and fingerprints. The Canadians also wanted a "determination whether Mengele is in fact wanted for war crimes."

There is nothing whatsoever about a Menke applying for a visa from Buenos Aires to enter Canada as a "landed immigrant" as was claimed by the Simon Wiesenthal Center.

The remaining unreleased documents, Senator D'Amato's office told me on February 25, 1985 probably originated with the Netherlands and the British, having nothing whatsoever to do with a "Menke" emigrating to Canada.

The Rabbi and the Senator

The combined efforts of Senator D'Amato and Rabbi Hier to force release of the four denied documents from the U.S. Army FOI Office is of significance. Just before they formed their alliance, the widely syndicated columnist, Jack Anderson, had revealed (Jan. 14, 1985) that D'Amato had been among several "distinguished members of Congress" who had intervened to stop the deportation of the Estonian war criminal, Karl

Linnas (see *Deportation Cases*).

D'Amato had responded to requests of the so-called Joint Baltic Committee of the Assembly of Captive European Nations (ACEN) which sought Congressional help in barring Linnas's deportation to the U.S.S.R. after he was found guilty of having concealed his war crimes as commandant of an Estonian concentration camp.

The ostensible basis for barring such a move was stated by D'Amato in a letter of September 28, 1984 to the U.S. Secretary of State, George Shultz. America's policy of non-recognition of the Soviet Baltic states, D'Amato maintained, would be "outright violated" by the deportation.

The ACEN official, one Dr. Edward Rubel, who had elicited D'Amato's support in behalf of Linnas, wrote to Secretary of State George Shultz charging the OSI with being a front for "Jewish Zionists" and agents of the Soviet KGB. Rubel, Anderson disclosed, wrote that Baltic Jews who did manage to escape the Nazi invaders and join Partisans to fight the Nazis were "leaders of extermination battalions, killing innocent people and burning their abodes."

Actually, D'Amato's action in behalf of Linnas had been detected before Anderson's January exposé. On December 19, 1984, D'Amato sent a note to Secretary Shultz claiming that "some individuals may have misinterpreted my letter to you...as an attempt to protect Nazi war criminals... I find such interpretations outrageous...It is inconceivable that Nazi war criminals should seek protection under our captive nation policy."

When the Anderson column did appear, an uproar ensued. Furthermore D'Amato faced an election year and what the New York *Daily News* called (Jan. 16, 1985) the loss of "the potent Jewish vote."

When Rabbi Hier was denied four of the released Mengele documents, the Wiesenthal official and D'Amato "joined forces" to sue for the release of the foreign government-originated materials.

Crying that he was "lied to, pure and simple" by the ACEN émigrés, D'Amato now became vocal in demanding that "war criminals must be deported..." (*The Jewish Ledger,* Jan. 31, 1985).

Immediately, Hier as well as other Jewish leaders, sprang to D'Amato's defense saying that the Senator had been "duped"; that the entire affair was "an obvious misunderstanding," according to Nathan Perlmutter, director of the Anti-Defamation League (ADL).

Declared Malcolm Hoenlein, executive director, the Jewish Community Relations Council: "Senator D'Amato's record with regard to the prosecution of Nazi war criminals has been consistently supportive...

There is no question as to [his] conviction and motivation."

The facts of the D'Amato record in the Senate on the prosecution of Nazi war criminals indicate no active affirmation of this issue prior to the Mengele-Linnas episode.

Overlooked by all commentators was the long-established fact that the Assembly of Captive European Nations (ACEN) — at whose behest D'Amato originally intervened for the war criminal Linnas — was first financed in 1949 with covert CIA funding as this writer and other journalists have demonstrated.

In Washington, D.C., U.S. Attorney General William French Smith announced that the OSI would "launch a full-scale investigation" into the Mengele matter: Senator D'Amato demanded "immediate action!"

CIA On Mengele: Drug Dealer

Following release of the Canadian document, the CIA then checked in with its documents on Mengele. Senator D'Amato's press aide, Gary Lewi, told me on February 26, 1985: "And just wait till you see the CIA documents. What they gave us. Most of them deleted out of existence. Worthless! No analysis pages or nothing!"

Not altogether. Some of the 17 documents released by the CIA are of more than passing interest. As *The New York Times* reported on Feb. 26th, most of these materials consist of reports on Mengele's involvement in illegal drug trafficking.

The period covered by the CIA materials runs from a cable dated 6 June 1972 through late 1979. The first dated document is a cable describing a drug operation from a farm owned by a person named Mengele but using the name "Dr. Henrique Wollman." Was this the wanted Auschwitz criminal, the CIA agent asked CIA headquarters in Langley, Virginia. The CIA's source in Latin America was "a petty criminal" and the material itself was "unevaluated."

The CIA received a follow-up report "confirming" the individual as Josef Mengele. However, the farm's location was moved a few hundred miles closer to the Brazilian border and the doctor became an "auto mechanic."

By 1979, the CIA had dug deeper into Mengele's drug dealings. A cable asks for detailed information on the Latin American subsidiaries of the family's company, Mengele & Son, hypothesizing that it "could serve as a mechanism to move or launder large sums of money as well as to cover the movement of illicit narcotics."

These cables were widely disseminated throughout the government: Drug Enforcement Agency (DEA), Treasury, Defense Intelligence Agency (DIA), State Department, and the FBI were among the recipients.

It is important to underscore the oft-demonstrated fact that Nazi war criminals with active political networks and terror operations in Latin America have in part financed their operations by way of drug trafficking, counterfeit money rings and small arms sales to any national buyer.

The most relevant and recent example is that of Klaus Barbie who often operated precisely in this fashion.

Missing from the equation is the demonstrated fact that among the world's largest dealers in illicit drug dealing is the CIA itself. A serious, scholarly study by Alfred W. McCoy titled *The Politics of Heroin in Southeast Asia* (1972) offers extensive documentation of the CIA's "rogue elephant" (illegal) undertakings financed with the liquid cash of drug dealing. The Church Committee's findings in the U.S. Senate also supplied prima facie data on this vital point.

Mengele and Bormann

The CIA also carried unevaluated reports about Mengele during the 1972-1979 period as shown by these 17 documents. He was supposed to have had plastic surgery in 1974, making him look younger than his then 63 years. Another report detailed his purported meetings with Martin Bormann, another major war criminal who was found guilty *in absentia* of crimes against humanity during the Nuremberg war crimes trials.

According to a June 7, 1974 CIA report on Mengele "circa 1968... Martin Bormann was then living with Mengele...in Paraguay..."

The dates of these unevaluated reports — raw field materials, in the view of this writer — suggest that the CIA source for the Bormann connection may have been the late Ladislas Farago, the 1974 best-selling author of *Aftermath, The Final Search for Martin Bormann* an extravagantly undocumented jumble.

Forensic evidence developed by West German authorities in 1973 — and accepted by a special tribunal examining the matter of Bormann's death — showed with "probability bordering on certainty" that the Nazi Party Secretary died — either by suicide or Soviet gunfire — early on May 2, 1945.

Farago had been claiming in the pages of sensationalistic British tabloids through the early 1970's that he "found" Bormann alive in Latin America — and living with Mengele. (Farago's dispatches for the London *Daily*

Express were considered "useless" by the West German court.)

Another Nazi hunter also figures with Bormann's case.

Simon Wiesenthal had declared Bormann was alive from the late 1950's through the late 1960's. A UPI story of March 13, 1968 quoted Wiesenthal as having told a Swedish newspaper that he and co-workers had "tracked down" Bormann to a Brazilian hamlet on the Paraguayan border.

Wiesenthal was interrogated on September 29, 1970 under oath before a magistrate of the Criminal Investigation Division of the Provincial Court in Vienna. The Nazi hunter admitted in his court statement that "until recently I have made statements to several journalists regarding the conjectural whereabouts of Martin Bormann."

While backing away from his previous categorical assertions about Bormann, Wiesenthal swore under oath: "In other words, at no time during a questioning — and that goes for my interrogation today [in Vienna] — could I or can I say how I might be in a position to represent with certainty that the accused [war criminal, Bormann] was at this particular place."

Despite his curiously obtuse jargon, Wiesenthal as a matter of practice — during TV appearances in the United States during the late 1970's, for example — has always been quick to assure one and all that "Bormann is dead!"

Ladislas Farago never did cease making extravagant sums from his tales about Bormann and Mengele. Of significance is his May 17, 1978 letter to the Subcommittee on Immigration regarding its hearings planned that year for investigating U.S. intelligence utilization of alleged Nazi war criminals and collaborators.

Both the Congressional hearings and 1978 GAO report were useless and "wasteful of taxpayer's money," Farago wrote. In his letter he "proudly" admitted his former employment as a CIA operative for Radio Free Europe (RFE) and argued how "exceptionally valuable" a former Hungarian Nazi general (a secret police agent who had collaborated with the Gestapo and was wanted by Hungary for war crimes) was to Farago during his days of service with the CIA.

Mengele, Josef, born March 16, 1911, Guenzburg/Son., Germany. NSDAP #317885. SS #5574974. Promoted to Hpt'stuf. (*Hauptsturmfuehrer,* Captain), April 20, 1943, honoring birth date of Adolf Hitler. Source: Berlin Document Center, List of SS Officers.

In arguing for the employment of some former Nazis, Farago went on to state "they [former Nazis] could have been [useful]... at a time when the CIA and FBI were still our first line of defense, even as they would be today, if dopes, dupes and Soviet agents in our midst had not conspired to destroy their full effectiveness."

In yet another missive — this time to President Jimmy Carter, dated April 23, 1978 — Farago asserted: "I am a Jew, a survivor of the Holocaust."

In a telephone call to the Subcommittee during the week of July 18, 1978, Farago denounced the Hearings about to take place, according to a Congressional source.

On the same day that the CIA documents — not one of which dealt with the vital 1949-1970 period — were released, the Simon Wiesenthal Center announced through its general counsel, Martin Mendelsohn, formerly of the OSI, that it was offering a $1 million reward for information leading to the capture and extradition of Dr. Josef Mengele.

Cautionary Warnings

In the midst of the latest Mengele upheaval, there were other cautionary developments. The Washington bureau of *The Daily News* of New York (Feb. 19, 1985) sought out Neal Sher, OSI director, in an attempt to pin down precisely what, if anything, his "full-scale" probe could accomplish.

First, Sher said, "we've got to find out if the U.S. had any involvement with Mengele." Then, he said, "We'll do whatever we can to locate the guy."

Assume, the *Daily News* put to Sher, that you do locate Mengele, then what can you actually do? "There's not much more than [sic] we can say," Sher replied.

The newspaper quoted an unnamed "career official in the Justice Department" who pointed out that his agency "has little power and virtually no authority to hunt down [Nazi war] criminals in foreign countries."

Added *The News*: "The career official... viewed [Attorney General William French] Smith's announcement, made at the same time an international panel [of Auschwitz survivors] in Israel was conducting hearings on Mengele's war activities, as primarily political."

In Jerusalem, the founder of Israel's intelligence, Mossad, Issar Harel — who commanded the special team that sought out, located, abducted in Argentina and brought to trial Adolf Eichmann in 1960 — warned against the mounting hysteria over Mengele.

Harel told how the Mossad had checked out Mengele's whereabouts during the Eichmann operation but without success. He pointed out that professional intelligence agents had confirmed sightings of Mengele over the years since 1953 in Argentina and Paraguay but they never engaged in public "media displays."

The JTA reported from Jerusalem on February 6, 1985 that "Harel was critical of persons who announce they know where the death camp doctor is. The search for Mengele should be carried out quietly, he said."

On the proviso that his name would not be used, a former analyst, now retired from the CIA was asked by me to assess the latest Mengele uproar.

"Anybody slightly familiar with that case," the ex-CIA intelligence evaluator told me, "knows that all this hoopla — a lot of it motivated by political and personal ego-tripping — is not going to nail Mengele. Did Harel and his team hold a press conference before going in to Argentina?

"These self-styled 'Nazi hunters' are among the worst of the lot. Take a close look at Harel's book about how he and the Mossad team captured Eichmann [the book is *The House on Garibaldi Street*, published in 1975, CRA].

"You will not find one line about Simon Wiesenthal who never tires of telling the press how he tracked down Eichmann and gave his materials to the Israelis. He takes credit for Eichmann!

"In his book, Harel does in fact give elaborate credit to Dr. Fritz Bauer, the West German prosecutor, who provided Mossad with the basic documentation and personal leads that were needed for the Eichmann operation.

"Let's see what the OSI can come up with. Then we can go on from there. If anyone's doing really serious work on going after Mengele, you can bet you won't hear about it until after it's over."

Right Wing Drive Against OSI

Since its inception, both the Ultra Right and the Respectable Right have attacked the OSI with the strategic purpose of eliminating the unit.

The Thunderbolt, official publication (15,000 circulation) of the National States Right Party whose origins are largely Ku Klux Klan in Georgia, screamed in its November 1982 issue that "radical Jews founded the OSI" in order to send "elderly Anti-Communist Patriotic East Europeans" back to face rigged Soviet courts and "certain execution" for "fighting Communists during World War II...JUST AS ALL AMERICANS SHOULD HAVE AT THAT TIME!"

Other elements of the Klan and various Nazi Party offshoots — most with small membership, all advocates/practitioners of violence against Blacks, Jews, liberals and communists — have raised defense funds for charged war criminals (John Demjanjuk, for example, see *Deportations*) and have mounted anti-Semitic demonstrations at OSI trials in Chicago, Cleveland, Boston, Los Angeles and Florida.

These blatantly racist voices are echoed, in turn, by the more sophisticated attacks launched against OSI from the so-called "Institute for Historical Review," the "Revisionists" who give wide circulation to their outrageous falsehoods that the Holocaust was a "Jew Communist hoax," that there was no Final Solution and Auschwitz was a bakery. Such patent lies are expensively endowed with a seeming "scholarship."

Spearhearding this effort — which goes far beyond the reach of the Ultras of "gutter fascism" — has been the 325,000 paid circulation of *Spotlight*, issued by what some experts believe is the country's largest anti-Semitic group, the Liberty Lobby in Washington, D.C. which enjoys numerous and often influential Congressional contacts who are not well disposed toward OSI, for example Sen. Jesse Helms (R-NC).

Spotlight has carried large features defending such genocidists as Demjanjuk, Linnas, Fedorenko and Laipenieks.

More ominous clouds on the horizon of OSI's immediate future may be seen in certain Eastern European and Soviet emigré organizations that exercise considerable voting power in the ethnic urban centers of the country. Already a so-called Free Baltic Committee successfully persuaded ranking U.S. Senators to intervene in behalf of the war criminal Linnas, scheduled for deportation possibly to Soviet Estonia (see *Deportation*). Leaders of some of these emigré groups have been linked to the Assembly of Captive European Nations (ACEN), known to have been originally financed by the CIA since 1949 (see *The Mengele Case*).

In 1985, President Ronald Reagan appointed the syndicated Right-wing columnist, Pat Buchanan, as White House director of communications. Buchanan has waged incessant warfare against the OSI, calling for its liquidation from his columns and on national TV.

Washington observers also feel that the installation of another arch-conservative ideologue, Edwin Meese, 3d as U.S. Attorney General — along with the Buchanan influence in Chief Executive circles — may well strengthen the growing menace to the OSI during the lame duck years of the Reagan administration.

That the attack against OSI from the Right has intensified to a serious level is clear.

Unfinished Business

At mid-1985, the following matters have in no way been conclusively followed through by various agencies of the U.S. government:

- The GAO's (General Accounting Office) report on U.S. intelligence utilization of Nazi war criminals and charges of cover-ups of such usage. Underway since 1982.
- The Subcommittee on Immigration of the Judiciary Committee of the U.S. House of Representatives has not held hearings on the charges assigned to the GAO for impartial investigation since 1978.
- Notwithstanding the OSI and U.S. Attorney General's 1983 assurances that the case of Robert Jan (Jean) Verbelen would be fully investigated and reported by the OSI, this has not been done.
- The OSI report on the Josef Mengele matter will remain unresolved until its full release to the public (much in the format of the 1983 report on Klaus Barbie).
- Six Nazi war criminals have been deported to date, according to the OSI; a dozen deportations may become final by end of 1985. Not a single Nazi war criminal has ever been *deported back to the soil on which his crimes were committed.*
- According to the claims of OSI director, Neal Sher, there are "over 300 cases" which can be developed for triability of identifiable Nazi war criminals yet living in the United States. How many, what percentage of this *OSI-estimated* number will be prosecuted?

What Background Material is Available?*

Books, Booklets, Anthologies, Monographs and Theses
(alphabetical by author)

- Allen, Charles R. Jr., *Nazi War Criminals Among Us,* (Jewish Currents, New York, N.Y. 1963). (Out of print. See local libraries.)
- Allen, Charles R. Jr. and Rochelle Saidel-Wolk, *Nazi War Criminals in America: Facts... Action,* (Charles R. Allen Jr. Productions Inc., Albany, N.Y. 1981).
- Allen, Charles R. Jr., *Nazi War Criminals in America: Facts... Action, The Basic Handbook,* (Highgate House, N.Y. 1985).
- Allen, Charles R. Jr., *The Politics of Nazi Genocide and Its Socio-Economic Base,* published as a 5-part series by *Martyrdom and Resistance*, organ of The American Federation of Jewish Fighters, Camp Inmates and Nazi Victims, New York, Dec. 1982 - Dec. 1983. (Eli Zborowski, Editor-in-Chief, Dr. Harvey Rosenfeld, Editor. In its 12th year, *M&R* has become a valuable research source.) The Federation is the largest survivors' organization in the Western Hemisphere. Also presented in full as a Paper read before The New York Society of Clinical Psychologists at the Ferkauf Graduate School of Yeshiva University in New York City, April 29, 1982 upon the occasion of The Society's presentation of its Fourth Annual Holocaust Memorial Award to Mr. Allen for his "extraordinarily insightful writings and courage in the unrelenting struggle against fascism wherever it may appear." (This Paper will be issued in 1985 as a monograph and may be ordered through the publishers of this book.)
- Allen, Charles R. Jr., *The Nuremberg Processes and the Presence of Accused Nazi War Criminals and Collaborators in the United States,* a Paper delivered before the Philadelphia Bar Association, October 16, 1978, Philadelphia, Pa. (The Paper was also delivered at Temple University Law School, October 17, 1978, Philadelphia, Pa.)
- Allen, Charles R. Jr., Vol. I, *From Hitler to Uncle Sam: How American Intelligence Used Accused Nazi War Criminals, A Documentation and Commentary,* Illustrated with Appendices, (Highgate House, N.Y.) Forthcoming 1985.
- Allen, Charles R. Jr., Vol. II, *A Nation Indicted: America's Nazi War*

---

* Titles of all publications in this section are set in bold face italic type whereas similar titles are just italicized elsewhere. The listings here are intended to provide convenience for the reader as researcher.

Criminals — History, A Documentation — and A Theoretical Analysis, (Highgate House, N.Y.) Forthcoming.
- Allen, Charles R. Jr., (see under Tillem, Ivan L., below).
- Blum, Howard, **Wanted! The Search for Nazis in America**, (Quadrangle/The New York Times Book Co., New York, N.Y. 1977).
- Bower, Tom, **The Pledge Betrayed, America and Britain and the Denazification of Post-War Germany,** (Doubleday, N.Y. 1982).
- Bower, Tom, **Klaus Barbie, The Butcher of Lyons** (Pantheon, N.Y. 1984).
- Dabringhaus, Erhard, **Klaus Barbie**, (Acropolis Books, Washington, D.C. 1984).
- Hanusiak, Michael, **Lest We Forget**, (Progress Books, Toronto, Canada, 1976; 1982 English, Ukrainian and German editions). (Mr. Hanusiak is the editor of **The Ukrainian News**, a weekly published at 85 E. 4th St., New York, N.Y. 10003. The paper regularly carries reports on the issue of Ukrainian war criminals in the United States and Canada.)
- Higham, Charles, **Trading with the Enemy, An Exposé of the Nazi-American Money Plot 1933-1949,** (Delacorte Press, N.Y. 1983).
- Higham, Charles, **America's Swastikas,** (Doubleday, N.Y. 1985).
- Infield, Glenn B., **Skorzeny, Hitler's Commando,** (St. Martin's Press, N.Y. 1981).
- Lasby, Clarence G., **Project Paperclip,** (Atheneum, New York, N.Y. 1975).
- Littman, Sol, **War Criminal On Trial, The Rauca Case,** (Lester & Orpen Dennys, Toronto, Canada 1983).
- Loftus, John, **The Belarus Secret**, as edited by Nathan Miller, (Knopf, N.Y. 1982).
- Morse, Arthur D., **While Six Million Died**, (Hart Publishing Co., New York, N.Y. 1967).
- Rabner, Stuart, **A Commitment Compromised: The Treatment of Nazi War Criminals by the U.S. Government.** An undergraduate thesis, 1982 (copyrighted) on file at the library of the Woodrow Wilson School, Princeton University, Princeton, N.J.
- Ryan, Allan A. Jr., **Quiet Neighbors: The True Story of Nazi War Criminals in America,** (Harcourt Brace Jovanovich, N.Y. 1984).
- Saidel, Rochelle, G., **The Outraged Conscience: Seekers of Justice for Nazi War Criminals in America**, (State University of New York Press, Albany, N.Y. 1984).

- Tillem, Ivan L., Editor, *The Jewish Directory and Almanac, 1984, A Compendium of Judaica,* (Pacific Press, N.Y. 1984). A large section titled "Nazi War Criminals in the United States" features the writings of Charles R. Allen, Jr., and reprints in part *Nazi War Criminals in America: Facts...Action* by Mr. Allen and Rochelle G. Saidel. (The book may be ordered through the publishers at Suite 1005, 310 Madison Ave., New York, N.Y. 10017. $11.95 per copy plus $1.50 p & h.)

Major Magazine and Newspaper Articles
(alphabetical by author)

- "Nazi War Criminals Among Us" by Charles R. Allen, Jr. Classic series published in Jan., Feb., Mar. 1963 by *Jewish Currents* magazine, 22 East 17th St., N.Y., N.Y. 10003. (Later issued with addenda as *Nazi War Criminals Among Us*, 1963, 1964.)
- "Our Government 'Replies' to Charges," by Charles R. Allen Jr., *Jewish Currents,* March, 1963. (With addenda to new findings re Nazi criminals in U.S.: 1964-1968.)
- "Hubertus Strughold, Nazi in U.S.A.: 'Father of American Space Medicine'," by Charles R. Allen, Jr., *Jewish Currents*, Dec., 1974.
- "The Strange Case of V.D. Samarin: Nazi Collaborator at Yale," by Charles R. Allen, Jr., *Jewish Currents*, Nov., 1976.
- "Twisted Tales and Trails: Odyssey of a Nazi Collaborator" (The Soobzokov Matter), by Charles R. Allen, Jr., *Jewish Currents*, Dec., 1977; "Allen Replies to Soobzokov's Lawyer," *Jewish Currents,* March, 1978.
- "Pursue the Bitter Past for a Better Future," by Charles R. Allen, Jr., *Newsday* syndicate, Feb. 24, 1977 *(The Washington Post, Los Angeles Times).* Estimated readers: 6 million.
- "Nazi War Criminals in the United States," by Charles R. Allen, Jr., *The Jewish Veteran,* Sept., 1979, publication of the Jewish War Veterans of the U.S.A.
- "U.S. Passport for Genocide," by Charles R. Allen, Jr., *Reform Judaism,* Sept., 1980, publication of the Union of American Hebrew Congregations, 838 Fifth Ave., N.Y., N.Y. 10021.
- "Wanted! For Crimes Against Humanity," *Keeping Posted,* Vol. XXVI, No. 1, Oct. 1980, published by the Union of American Hebrew Congregations, New York, N.Y. "A Passport for Genocide," by Charles R. Allen, Jr., (entire issue deals with Nazi war criminals in America).

- "OSI vs Nazi War Criminals: Success or Failure?" by Charles R. Allen, Jr., ***Reform Judaism***, May, 1981.
- "Dealing with War Criminals in the U.S., The Question of Deportation," by Charles R. Allen, Jr., ***JTA (Jewish Telegraphic Agency)***, 3-part series, carried world-wide by JTA subscribers and, additionally, other wire services abroad, Feb. 12, 13, 14, 1982. (Major Anglo-Jewish newspapers, including: ***The Jewish Advocate,*** Boston, Mass.; ***The Jewish Forward,*** New York, N.Y.; ***The Jewish Week,*** New York, N.Y.; ***The Jewish Press,*** New York, N.Y.; ***The Baltimore Jewish Times,*** Baltimore, Md.; ***The Jewish Week of Washington, D.C.***; ***The Detroit Jewish News,*** Detroit, Mich.; ***The Sentinel,*** Chicago, Ill.; ***The Jewish Light,*** St. Louis, Mo.; ***The Jewish Floridian,*** Miami, Fla.; ***The Philadelphia Jewish Exponent,*** Philadelphia, Pa.; ***The B'nai B'rith Messenger,*** Los Angeles, Calif.)
- "Where to Deport War Criminals," by Charles R. Allen, Jr., ***Jewish Currents,*** Sept. 1982.
- "America — A Refuge for War Criminals, U.S. Unwilling to Deport Nazis to Communist Nations," by Charles R. Allen, Jr., ***The Times Union,*** Albany, N.Y., and syndicated by the Hearst Newspapers. Oct. 10, 1982, Oct. 17, 1982.
- "A Case of Distortion, CBS '60 Minutes' and its 'Nazi Connection'," a 3-part series by Charles R. Allen, Jr., ***JTA (Jewish Telegraphic Agency),*** May 28, June 11 and June 18, 1982.
- "Give Me Your Tired, Your Poor... *Your Nazi War Criminals?* A Review of John Loftus' Allegations," Part I, by Charles R. Allen, Jr., ***The Jewish Veteran,*** Sept./Oct., 1982 (Magazine of the Jewish War Veterans of the U.S.A.).
- "Do the Deported Depart? Or Do Convicted Nazi War Criminals Continue to Live Freely Among Us?" Part II, by Charles R. Allen, Jr., Nov./Dec., 1982, ***The Jewish Veteran.***
- "Prosecuting Nazi War Criminals, Is Justice Being Obstructed?" by Charles R. Allen, Jr., ***Jewish Digest,*** Jan. 1983.
- "Klaus Barbie: Odyssey of the 'Butcher of Lyon'," a 3-part series by Charles R. Allen, Jr. I, "Barbie's Escape from Europe: The Vatican 'Monastery Routes,' the CIC and the International Red Cross," Feb.16, 1983; II, "Barbie Operated for Three Decades Under Orders of a Secret Underground SS Headed by Skorzeny," Feb. 17, 1983; III, "How Barbie Coordinated Nazi Activities in Latin America," Feb. 18, 1983. A worldwide release by the ***JTA (Jewish Telegraphic Agency),*** carried

in some 400 newspapers and magazines in more than 16 languages in 38 countries, cited widely by worldwide radio and TV. Estimated audience: 260 million. (For U.S. Anglo-Jewish press coverage, see partial listings above at "Dealing with War Criminals in the U.S., the Question of Deportation," *JTA,* by Charles R. Allen, Jr.)

- "The Justice Department's Report on Barbie Fails to Face Basic Issues," by Charles R. Allen, Jr., a *JTA* Special Report, Sept. 1-7, 1983.
- "Behind the Scenes of the U.S. Report on Barbie: What Was *Not* Put Into It," by Charles R. Allen, Jr., a *JTA* Special Report, Sept. 15, 1983.
- "Study by U.S. Defending Use of Barbie Is Unconvincing," an Op-Ed piece for the Cox Newspapers by Charles R. Allen, Jr., *The Miami News,* Miami, Fla., Nov. 2, 1983. Syndicated.
- "Vatican Helped Top Nazis Flee Europe, Jewish Magazine Says," AP (Associated Press), A-wire to all print, radio, TV subscribers worldwide, June 19, 1983, estimated audience: 500 million. (Allen's *Reform Judiasm* 1983-1984 series starts.)
- "The Vatican-Nazi Connection, Secret LaVista Report Reveals How Barbie and Other Nazi War Criminals Escaped Justice Via 'Monastery Routes'," by Charles R. Allen, Jr., Part I. *Reform Judaism,* Spring/Summer 1983, Vol. 11, No. 3.
- "The LaVista Report, Part II, The Vatican-Nazi Connection" by Charles R. Allen, Jr., with rebuttals of the Allen series by Roman Catholic historians, Dr. Eugene J. Fisher and Dr. George R. Kemon. *Reform Judaism,* Fall, 1983. Vol 12, No. 1.
- "Charles R. Allen, Jr. Replies to His Critics," III by Charles R. Allen, Jr., *Reform Judaism,* Winter 1983-1984, Vol. 12, No. 2.
- "Debate Rages: Did Vatican Help Nazis to Escape from Europe?" an Op-Ed debate. "U.S. Documents Attest to Clerical Involvement," by Charles R. Allen, Jr. and "Accusations Not Made in Good Faith" by Mons. John M. Osterreicher, *National Catholic Reporter,* Mar. 2, 1984, Vol. 20, No. 19.
- "The Verbelen Case: Klaus Barbie, American CIC & CIA," by Charles R. Allen, Jr., *JTA,* 3-part series, Jan. 24, 25 & 26, 1984. Worldwide transmission and pickup in Jewish press and daily media. Estimated readers: 16 million.

- "How *Not* to Pursue Nazi War Criminals in America, What's Wrong with The Belarus Secret," by Charles R. Allen, Jr., *Jewish Currents,* April 1984.

- "Why U.S. Monopoly Capitalism Imported Nazi War Criminals," by Charles R. Allen, Jr., *Israel Horizons,* May/June 1984, Vol. 23, Nos. 5/6.
- "A Lesson in Complicity as U.S. Lets Nazi War Criminal Avoid Justice," an Op-Ed piece by Charles R. Allen, Jr. *The Boston Globe,* Aug. 30, 1984. (Editorial excerpts, *The Los Angeles Times,* Sept. 1, 1984.)
- "An Urgent Goal," Special Feature, *JTA* 3-part series. In-Depth Critique of Simon Wiesenthal Center's press conference, "Walter Rauff, SS War Criminal, and The Vatican" by Charles R. Allen, Jr., Sept. 28, Oct. 5 and Oct. 12, 1984.
- "Audience Stirred by Talk on Vatican and Nazis," *The Baltimore Evening Sun,* Baltimore, Md., May 27, 1984.
- "The Wrong Man, The Trials of Frank Walus," by Michael Arndt, *Sunday*, The Chicago Tribune Magazine, Dec. 2, 1984.
- "Drive on Nazi Suspects a Year Later: No U.S. Legal Steps Have Been Taken," by Ralph Blumenthal, *The New York Times*, Nov. 23, 1974 and *The New York Times Service* worldwide, (Strughold case).
- "Vatican Is Reported to Have Furnished Aid to Fleeing Nazis," by Ralph Blumenthal, *The New York Times,* Jan. 26, 1984 and *The New York Times Service* syndication worldwide.
- "German-Born NASA Expert Quits U.S. to Avoid a War Crimes Suit," by Ralph Blumenthal, *The New York Times*, Oct. 18, 1984. And *The New York Times Service* worldwide, (Rudolph case).
- "Second Man Linked to Nazis Quits U.S.," by Ralph Blumenthal, *The New York Times*, Oct. 20, 1984. And *The New York Times Service* worldwide (Avdzej case).
- "A Dispute Erupts on Medical Prize, Liver Research Award Named for Doctor Linked to Tests on Prisoners of Nazis," by Ralph Blumenthal, *The New York Times*, Nov. 11, 1984.
- "Were These Men Killers for the Nazis?" by David Friend, *Life Magazine*, Feb., 1980.
- "The Hunt for Ivan the Terrible," (The Demjanjuk Case) by Mark Gottlieb, *Cleveland Magazine*, Nov., 1979, Cleveland, Ohio.
- "Klaus Barbie, The French and the Jews," by F. DuPlessix Gray, *Vanity Fair,* Oct., Nov. 1983.
- The occasional papers, memoranda and communications of the Harvard Jewish Law Students Association at Harvard Law School, Cambridge, Mass., 1979-1984 are useful resources. The HJLSA also

issues a newsletter *Law & Human Rights Reporter.*
- A Special Series on Suspected Nazis in the Upper Great Lakes area by Richard Kenyon of *The Milwaukee Journal,* Milwaukee, Wis., Sept. 18, 19, 21 and 22, 1983. (Mr. Kenyon's excellent investigative series deals with the case of Zanis Butkus, admitted erstwhile officer who was decorated by the Nazis for his service in the Latvian Waffen SS, and other persons from that region — unnamed — then under OSI probe as potential defendants.)
- "The Hunters and the Hunted," by Stephen Klaidman, *The Washington Post,* Oct. 24, 1976 (a seminal contribution to this issue).
- "The Nazi Hunters," by Stephen Klaidman, *Present Tense,* Winter, 1977 (a publication of The American Jewish Committee, New York, N.Y.).
- "Une Guerre Inachevée: Le Scandale de la Dispersion Nazie dans le Tiers-Monde," par Ignacio Klich, *Le Monde Diplomatique,* July 1983, No. 352, 14 pp.; Paris, France. (Cites extensively works of Charles R. Allen, Jr.)
- "The Silence Over Samarin," by Bob Lamm, *A Jewish Journal at Yale,* Summer, 1983, Vol. I, No. 1. Published by Yale Hillel Foundation, 1904A Yale Station, New Haven, CT 06520. An interpretive essay on the case of former Yale Faculty member, V.D. Samarin-Sokolov (see **Denaturalization Cases**).
- "Bishop Trifa: Prelate or Persecutor?" by Victor Livingston with Dennis DebBaudt, *Monthly Detroit,* July 1980, Detroit, Mich.
- "Nazi War Criminals: The Search and the Legal Process Continue," by Michael May, for the IJA (Institute of Jewish Affairs) in association with the World Jewish Congress, Mar. 4, 1983, No. 4 (copies may be obtained through World Jewish Congress, 1 Park Ave., New York, N.Y. 10016).
- "Denaturalizing a Treblinka Guard," by Stanley Mailman, *New York Law Journal,* Mar. 4, 1981, Vol. 185, No. 42.
- "Storm Behind the Nazi Case," by Ruth Marcus, *The National Law Journal,* Oct. 27, 1980, Vol. 3, No. 7.
- "U.S. Unit Stifled in Bid to Deport Suspected Nazis," by Dan Morain, *Los Angeles Times,* Los Angeles, Calif., Aug. 22, 1983.
- "Justice Department and Nazi Criminals," A Rebuttal by Allan A. Ryan, Jr. *The Boston Globe,* Sept. 17, 1984 (in answer to Charles R. Allen, Jr.'s Op-Ed piece, above).
- Author Rejoins Ryan: "State Department Not Aggressive on Nazi

Deportations, Says Congress." Letter by Charles R. Allen, Jr., *The Boston Globe,* Sept. 26, 1984.
- "The Simon Wiesenthal Center: State-of-the-Art Activism or Hollywood Hype?" A Special Report by Gary Rosenblatt, *Baltimore Jewish Times,* Sept. 14, 1984. A 14-page analysis by the editor of one of the ranking Anglo-Jewish newspapers in the United States. (Reprints of this in-depth report may be ordered: *Baltimore Jewish Times,* 9104 N. Charles St., Baltimore, Md. 21218. Price: 50¢ ea. plus p & h).
- "U.S. Government's Use of Nazi War Criminals," by Rochelle Saidel-Wolk, *Times-Outlook*, Jan. 1979, *JTA (Jewish Telegraphic Agency)* feature.
- "Yeshiva University Cancels Dinner to Honor J. Peter Grace, Industrialist and Sponsor of Nazi Criminal," "Allen Exposes I.G. Farben Connection," by Rochelle Saidel-Wolk, *JTA (Jewish Telegraphic Agency)*, June 7, 1981.
- "Former CIA Official Says Ex-Nazi's Role in Slave Labor Camp Should Be Overlooked in Return for His Later Contributions to U.S. Space Program," by Rochelle Saidel, *JTA (Jewish Telegraphic Agency)* Daily News Bulletin, Oct. 23, 1984.
- "Misrepresentation and Materiality in Immigration Law — Scouring the Melting Pot," by Irene Astrid Steiner, *Fordham Law Review,* Mar. 1980, No. 4, Vol. XLVIII, (cites works of Charles R. Allen, Jr.).
- "Barbie Called One of Many Ex-Nazis Aided by U.S.," by Michael Wise, Reuters International A-line (all worldwide subscribers), Feb. 19, 1983, (estimated audience: 250 million).

Television
- *The Hunt for Nazi War Criminals, Today in the U.S.A.* — The David Susskind Show, January, 1977 (2½ hours), syndicated (with Charles R. Allen, Jr.).
- *Good Morning, America,* ABC News, TV Network, August 10, 1978, with Hugh Downes of ABC, interviewing Charles R. Allen, Jr. about his Congressional testimony regarding Nazi war criminals and U.S. intelligence.
- *From Hitler to Uncle Sam: How American Intelligence Used Accused Nazi War Criminals*, Charles R. Allen, Jr./Rochelle Saidel-Wolk, © 1979 Charles R. Allen Jr. Productions Inc.
- *Escape From Justice: Nazi War Criminals in America*, ABC Network News, "Close-Up" aired January 13, 1980, (with Charles R. Allen, Jr.).

- *Alive and Well in the U.S.A.: Nazi War Criminals*, The World in Action, (WIA-TV Co., London, Manchester, England, 1980) (U.S.A., 1981 distribution), (with Charles R. Allen, Jr.).
- *Nazi War Criminals in America*, WTBS and Cable News Network, CNN (Ted Turner Cable), May 3, 1981, national syndication, (with Charles R. Allen, Jr., Elizabeth Holtzman and Allan A. Ryan, Jr.).
- *Nazi Connection,* CBS, "60 Minutes," May 16, 1982.
- *The Journal,* CBC-TV Network (Canadian Broadcasting Corp.) Société Radio-TV, Canada, April 7, 1983. A 30-minute interview with Charles R. Allen, Jr. regarding Nazi war criminals in Canada, with Barbara Frum.
- *Klaus Barbie and the Nazi Network,* "Nightline," with Ted Koppel, ABC News, April 22, 1983 (a 3-way simulcast from Bolivia, Washington and New York, off satellite, live w/Richard Threlkeld and John Martin of ABC News and Charles R. Allen, Jr.). (Transcripts may be ordered from Nightline, Box 234, Ansonia Sta., New York, N.Y. 10023, Show #510, @ $2 ea.)
- *The Klaus Barbie Matter,* BBC, "Panorama," July 4, 1983 (London, England, worldwide distribution).
- *Good Morning, America,* ABC News, TV Network, August 18, 1983, (with Charles R. Allen, Jr.).
- *Arthur Rudolph and Project Paperclip,* ABC News, "Nightline" with Ted Koppel, Oct. 18, 1984. In Washington: Ray Cline, former Deputy Director, CIA and Allan A. Ryan, Jr., former OSI Director; in New York: Charles R. Allen, Jr., Nazi War Criminal expert and author. (Show #889, Transcript may be ordered through "Nightline" address above.)
- *CBS, NBC and ABC Network News,* A.M. programs, Jan. 27, 1984, live interviews with Charles R. Allen, Jr., later news programs taped through Jan. 29, 1984 concerning Allen's writings on Vatican routes and escaped Nazi war criminals after World War II. All major cable networks, led by Ted Turner's CNN (Cable News Network) had running story over three day period. Worldwide TV, radio and print media reached estimated global audience of 1 billion.

Radio

During 1983-1984, radio began devoting more in-depth attention to the Nazi war criminal issue. As yet there have not been any full documentary treatments but a few of the better quality "talk shows" have paid serious

attention as the following indicate:
- The Al Angeloro Show, NBC Radio-AM, Network. Sunday, August 28, 1983, 1 hour. "How Good Is the U.S. Government's Report on Klaus Barbie?" (with Charles Higham in Los Angeles and Charles R. Allen, Jr. in NBC studios, New York).
- The Al Angeloro Show, NBC Radio-AM, Network. Sunday, Feb. 5, 1984, 1 hour. "Did the Vatican Help Fleeing Nazis Escape Justice?" (with Father Robert Graham, official Vatican spokesman on the Holocaust period, and Charles R. Allen, Jr.).
- The Studs Terkel Show, WFMT, Chicago, Ill. (with Charles R. Allen, Jr.), March 1984, (nationally syndicated).
- National Public Radio Network, Sondra Gaiz chats with Charles R. Allen, Jr. on "U.S. Intelligence, Nazi War Criminals," March 6; April 29, 1984 (2 hours).

Newspapers

(Noted below are newspapers — with specialists' by-lines — which have consistently published the best coverage of the subject over the past several years. Alphabetically listed.)

- *The Chicago Daily News* and *The Chicago Sun-Times*, by Charles Nicodemus and William Clements, Front Page Award winners for several original investigations on subject (Walus and Cenkus cases), 1978-1984.
- *The Star-Ledger*, (Newark, N.J., Newhouse Chain) by Herb Jaffe, prize-winning investigative reporter, 15-part series on Soobzokov, 1978-1979, an invaluable, in-depth study.
- *The New York Times*, by Ralph Blumenthal, original investigations into Trifa, Braunsteiner Ryan, Strughold, Laipenieks and Rudolph cases, 1973-1979, Vatican, 1984, Mengele, 1985, Paperclip Nazis, 1985.
- *The Los Angeles Herald-Examiner*, by Dan Morain, 1980-1984.
- *The Philadelphia Daily News*, by Frank Dougherty, in-depth investigations of Osidach, Kowalchuks, Trucis, Theodorovich and Shuk cases, 1978-1985.
- *The San Diego Evening Tribune*, by Bob Dorn, on Central Intelligence Agency (CIA) involvement in Laipenieks case, 1976-1977.
- *SoHo Weekly News*, (N.Y., N.Y.) by Richard Steiger, "Is an Ex-Nazi SS Officer Getting Away? The Trouble With Howard Blum's 'Wanted!'" (Soobzokov case), May 26, 1977.

- *The Miami Herald*, Miami, Florida by Cathy Lynn Grossman (Fedorenko case).
- *Miami News* by David Holmberg, Miami, Florida (Fedorenko case).
- *Fort Lauderdale Daily News* by George McEvoy, Fort Lauderdale, Florida (Fedorenko case).
- *The Times-Union*, (Albany, N.Y.) by Fredric U. Dicker, (Hazners case), 1977-1979.
- *JTA (Jewish Telegraphic Agency)* Murray Zuckoff, editor, (165 W. 46 St., New York, N.Y. 10036). Reportage by Milton Friedman, Joseph Polakoff, Kevin Freeman, Rochelle Saidel. Since 1978, the most complete wire service/press coverage on the subject and an indispensable research source.
- *The World Union Press*, David Horowitz, editor. (The United Nations, New York, N.Y. 10017) Original contributions, especially on Trifa and Koreh cases, by an early specialist.
- *The Detroit Jewish News*, Philip Slomovitz, editor. Files constitute a running history of the issue. Editor Slomovitz was a pioneer on this issue.
- *The Chicago Sentinel,* J.I. Fishbein, editor. Early and consistent coverage, led by editor Fishbein.
- *The B'nai B'rith Messenger,* (Los Angeles, Calif.) The late editor, Joseph Jonah Cummins, and present publisher, Gilbert E. Thompson, have investigated and chronicled the issue since 1949.
- *Morgen Freiheit,* (New York, N.Y.) an early source (in Yiddish and English editions), M.E. Chaim Suller.

Anglo-Jewish Newspapers

The following newspapers have over the years provided consistent, accurate and up-to-date coverage and comment. Their files are most valuable. Alphabetically listed:

- *The Albany Jewish World,* Albany, N.Y. Editor: Samuel Clevenson.
- *The American Jewish Ledger,* Newark, N.J. Editor: Simon Bloom.
- *The Baltimore Jewish Times,* Baltimore, Md. Editor: Gary Rosenblatt.
- *The B'nai B'rith Messenger,* Los Angeles, Calif. Editor: Gilbert E. Thompson.
- *The Boston Jewish Advocate,* Boston, Mass. Editor: Bernard Hyatt.
- *The Buffalo Jewish Review,* Buffalo, N.Y. Editor: Harlan C. Abbey.
- *The Chicago Sentinel,* Chicago, Ill. Editor: J.I. Fishbein.
- *The Cleveland Jewish News,* Cleveland, Ohio. Editor: Cynthia

Dettelbach. (This newspaper issued an excellent special, "A Moment in History, the Demjanjuk Trial in Cleveland, Ohio," an original 1981 work. May be ordered care of the paper at 13910 Cedar Rd., Cleveland, Ohio 44118, @ 35¢ ea. plus p & h.)
- *The Detroit Jewish News,* Detroit, Mich. Editorship: Philip Slomovitz.
- *The Intermountain Jewish News,* Denver, Col. Editor: Miriam Goldberg.
- *The Jewish Daily Forward,* New York, N.Y. Editor: Simon Weber.
- *The Jewish Exponent,* Philadelphia, Pa. Editor: Al Erlich.
- *The Jewish Floridian Newspapers,* Miami, Fla. Editor: Fred Shochet.
- *The Morning Freiheit,* New York, N.Y. Managing Editor: Chaim Suller.
- *Northern California Jewish Bulletin,* San Francisco, Calif. Editor: Marc S. Klein (former editor, *The Exponent*).
- *The St. Louis Jewish Light,* St. Louis, Mo. Editor: Robert A. Cohen.

Anglo-Jewish Magazines

Among those magazines concerned with Jewish affairs, the following have carried important contributions:

- *Jewish Currents,* New York, N.Y. Editor: Morris U. Schappes.
- *Keeping Posted,* New York, N.Y. Editors: Aron Hirt-Manheimer; Steven Schnur.
- *Moment,* Boston, Mass. Editor: Leonard Fein.
- *Present Tense,* New York, N.Y. Editor: Murray Polnar.
- *Reform Judaism,* New York, N.Y. Editor: Aron Hirt-Manheimer; M.E. Steven Schnur.

U.S. Government Hearings and Publications

Between 1974 and 1979, the House Judiciary Subcommittee on Immigration held a number of hearings on the issue of Nazi war criminals in America. Note especially the following sources:

- *Alleged Nazi War Criminals — Hearings before the Subcommittee on Immigration, Citizenship, and International Law of the Committee on the Judiciary, House of Representatives, Ninety-Fifth Congress*, Part I — Aug. 3, 1977, Serial No. 95-39; Part II — July 19-21, 1978, Serial No. 39 (U.S. Government Printing Office, Washington, D.C. 20548).
- *Report by the Comptroller General of the United States: Wide-*

spread Conspiracy to Obstruct Probes of Alleged Nazi War Criminals Not Supported by Available Evidence — Controversy May Continue, (U.S. General Accounting Office, Washington, D.C., May 15, 1978).
- ***Klaus Barbie and the United States Government,*** A Report to the Attorney General of the United States (Washington, D.C., Aug. 16, 1983) in two volumes, by Allan A. Ryan Jr., Special Assistant to the Ass't. Attorney General, U.S. Justice Department.

Action: What Can You Do?

Educate all members of your community — non-Jewish and Jewish — about Nazi war criminals in America. The issue should be on the agenda of every concerned organization, including churches and synagogues, civic and veteran groups, Jewish Federations and community relations committees. If you are affiliated with any such organizations, suggest speakers, seminars or audio-visuals about the topic. Urge that the issue be explored in high school and college Holocaust classes. (Since the first edition of this handbook, colleges have started special courses on this subject using ***Nazi War Criminals in America — Facts...Action! The Basic Handbook*** as the basis for a syllabus.) Contact your local media — radio, television and newspapers — to cover this breaking story. (To order copies of ***The Basic Handbook,*** see order form, p. 111.)

Find out if there are any Nazi war criminals or organizations in your area, and organize appropriately lawful and peaceful action. In addition, search out witnesses to atrocities committed by Nazi war criminals now living here. If a deportation or denaturalization hearing is held in your area, encourage lawful and proper attendance. This serves the two-fold purpose of educating community members and providing moral support for survivor-witnesses. (Witnesses from Europe, U.S.S.R., Israel and elsewhere may also appreciate efforts by your community to welcome them and provide hospitality.) Express your concern to pertinent government officials (listed on the following pages).

What Individuals and Organizations Should You Contact?

U.S. Government Officials
- President of the United States
  The White House
  Washington, D.C. 20500
- Your Congressperson
  House Office Building
  Washington, D.C. 20515
- Your Senators
  Senate Office Building
  Washington, D.C. 20510
- Office of the Director
  Office of Special Investigations
  (OSI)
  Suite 195
  1377 K St., N.W.
  Washington, D.C. 20005
  (202) 633-2502
- Members of the Judiciary Subcommittee on Immigration, Refugees and International Law,
  U.S. House of Representatives:
  Rep. Romano Mazzoli, Chairman (D-Ky)
  Rep. George Crockett (D-Mich)
  Rep. Hamilton Fish, Jr. (R-NY)
  Rep. Barney Frank (D-Mass)
  Rep. Sam Hall (D-Tex)
  Rep. Dan Ludgren (R-Calif)
  Rep. Bill McCollum (R-Fla)
  Rep. Larry Smith (D-Fla)
  House Office Building
  Washington, D.C. 20515
  Subcommittee telephone:
  (202) 225-5727

  Rep. Peter W. Rodino, Jr., Chairman
  Judiciary Committee
  Rayburn House Office Building
  Washington, D.C. 20515
  (202) 225-3436

National Organizations
- Office of the National Commander
  AMVETS
  1710 Rhode Island Avenue N.W.
  Washington, D.C. 20036
  (202) 223-9550
- Office of the National Commander
  Jewish War Veterans of the U.S.A.
  1811 R St., N.W.
  Washington, D.C. 20009
  (202) 265-6280
- Rabbi Paul B. Silton, Chairman
  Holocaust Survivors and Friends In Pursuit of Justice
  Temple Israel
  600 New Scotland Avenue
  Albany, N.Y. 12208
  (518) 438-7858
- Mr. Phil Baum
  American Jewish Congress
  15 E. 84 Street
  New York, N.Y. 10028
  (212) TR 9-4500

- Mr. Abraham Spiegel, Chairman
  Martyrs Memorial Museum
  of the Holocaust
  6505 Wilshire Blvd.
  Los Angeles, Calif. 90048
  (213) 852-1234
- Mr. Abraham J. Bayer
  National Jewish Community
  Relations Advisory Council
  443 Park Avenue South
  New York, N.Y. 10016
  (212) 684-6950
- Mr. Albert J. Abrams
  National Association of
  Jewish Legislators
  45 Thorndale Road
  Slingerlands, N.Y. 12159
  (518) 439-9597
- Mr. Elliot Welles
  Nazi War Criminals Desk
  Anti-Defamation League
  823 United Nations Plaza
  New York, N.Y. 10017
  (212) 490-2525
- Mr. David Geller
  American Jewish Committee
  165 E. 56 Street
  New York, N.Y. 10022
  (212) PL 1-4000

International Organizations
- Mr. Elan Steinberg,
  Public Information Director
  The World Jewish Congress
  1 Park Ave.
  New York, N.Y. 10016
  (212) 679-0600
  (WJC's Institute of Jewish Affairs issues a series of high quality studies called *Research Report* that may be obtained through Mr. Steinberg.)

Local Organizations
- Mr. John Ranz
  The Generation After
  2747 Throop Avenue
  New York, N.Y. 10469
  (212) 231-5456

A Special Word

- Holocaust Survivors and Friends In Pursuit of Justice merits special comment. Founded in 1984 for a single, specific purpose, namely to educate the American people and the U.S. Congress so as to make certain that Nazi war criminals ordered to deportation by American courts are sent back: 1) primarily and preferably to face justice at trials on the soil of the countries where they committed their crimes; or, 2) where they are wanted for those war crimes; or, 3) failing all else, to be extradited to Israel to face trial. At an extraordinary 3-day conference held in April 1984 at Temple Israel in Albany, N.Y. some 1,500 men, women and children from ten states and Canada — including 269 survivors of the Holocaust — launched this independent effort. Holocaust Survivors and Friends is committed to its task "until the last Nazi war criminal is tried and ordered deported from America's shores." This ad hoc effort is a unique organization; no other group in the United States has such a purpose.

In Praise of:
Nazi War Criminals in America: Facts... Action

The 1981 predecessor of 1985's *The Basic Handbook* reaped a stout harvest of praise and comment from all sectors: the media, educators, scholars, authors, activists, religious figures across the spectrum. A few are excerpted here:

The Media — Press

"An invaluable handbook. Excellent for beginners... very helpful for the already initiated. I constantly use it."
>Ralph Blumenthal, Investigative Reporter/Writer
>***The New York Times***

"World War II Nazis who fled Europe to America are unfinished business — a business that too many now prefer to forget. But the hard truth of the problem is concisely focused in a compendium called 'Nazi War Criminals in America: Facts... Action.' Only Nazi historian, sleuth and author Charles R. Allen, Jr. — in cooperation with Rochelle Saidel — is capable of producing so factual and well-researched a compendium, based on his meticulous and agonizing quest for the truth. Allen is a journalist's dream: a walking encyclopedia of facts concerning Nazi war criminals and collaborators, their movement and the blot they left on history... His new booklet is must-reading for anyone who seeks hard facts about the Nazi residue in America but even more so for those who have not forgotten the Nazi menace which yet threatens us all."
>Herb Jaffe, columnist, TV commentator
>and prize-winning investigative reporter of the
>***The Newark Star-Ledger***, Newark, N.J.
>(Newhouse Newspapers, largest readership of
>any chain in the United States)

"There is a much-underlined booklet down here (at denaturalization trials of accused Nazi war criminals) 'Nazi War Criminals in America: Facts... Action' that attracts a lot of attention...."
>**United Press International**
>Datelined West Palm Beach, Fla., Sept. 30, 1981

"It's quick, handy, accurate — and courageous! A handy weapon for everyone of us demanding justice!"
>David Horowitz, President, United Nations
>Correspondents Association

"You can't pretend to know anything about Nazi war criminals in America without this handbook... Get it, use it, spread it around."
Frederic U. Dicker, ***The New York Post***

"Here is the most definitive primer on the subject... Allen is undoubtedly the most knowledgeable writer in the country... A valuable resource guide for writers, researchers (and) should be read by all those concerned that justice has not taken place in this vital area."
Murray Waas, Special Correspondent
The Washington Post, The Nation, New Times

"The first reference of its kind... a veritable gold mine for those who want information about the criminals among us, Nazi war criminals that is.... It is amazing how much material has been crammed into this work... worth more than its weight in gold."
The Jewish Week, New York, Oct. 18, 1981

"An extremely important contribution to the effort to eradicate Nazism in America... a clear, concise, easy-to-read guide."
Robert A. Cohen, Editor
The Saint Louis Jewish Light
Past president, American Jewish Press Association

"A novel feature (of the booklet) is a section called 'Predicted Prosecutions' in which Allen lists 37 accused war criminals who had been the subject of a two-year inquiry and not put on trial. When Allen confronted (the U.S. Justice Department) with this and asked how come? he got a 'no-comment' but since then nine of the 37 have been put on trial."
Richard Yaffe, Editor, ***Israel Horizons***

"A significant contribution indeed.... No man has done more than Charles (Chuck) R. Allen, Jr. to expose U.S.-located Nazis... No one is more qualified..."
B'nai B'rith Messenger, Los Angeles, Calif., Aug. 14, 1981

"...most important!... should get the widest distribution among all people... There must be no relaxation on this question!"
Chaim Suller, M.E., ***Morning Freiheit,*** New York

"...very thorough... responsible... invaluable for the working press. Impressive job!"
The Journal, Poughkeepsie, N.Y.

"Very clever, very useful and very courageous!"
Edna Ruth Johnson, Editor, ***The Churchman***

Television and Radio

"The only serious, truly comprehensive work on this subject in the U.S. has been done by Allen, and he is the only one there that you must take seriously.... His booklet is a model of its kind."
John Ware, Producer, Writer, Investigative Reporter.
Granada T.V. International, England;
Producer, "The Hunt for Josef Mengele" (1978)

"My, oh my, that booklet is a tidy piece of dynamite! I use it time and again."
Michael Connor, ABC-TV Network News, Reporter on
"Escape from Justice: Nazi War Criminals in America" (1980)

"An extremely helpful, clever booklet. Invaluable and the people of Israel are grateful indeed for this contribution."
Judy Lessing, Commentator, KOL YISRAEL (1981)

Authors and Historians

"An invaluable tool for everyone connected with the news media and for everyone who writes and speaks on the subject and related concerns."
Yuri Suhl, **They Fought Back,**
The Story of Jewish Resistance in Europe

"Allen's anti-fascist writings reflect an extraordinary sensitivity, insight, compassion and brilliance. His intellectual leadership in providing a context for this particular issue (Nazi war criminals in the United States) is indispensable...."
The late Reuben Ainsztein, author of the monumental history,
Jewish Resistance In Nazi-Occupied Eastern Europe (1974).
Special correspondent, **The Times,** London, England

"The most concise presentation I've encountered. As long as mass murderers can ride our bureaucratic tape with impunity, the conscience of this country is stained with the blood of their victims...Allen's work will never let the world forget."
Vaughn Young, **The Interpol Connection** (1979)

"This is all very important for us here at the Archives. Researchers, historians, a generation hence, will be grateful to you."
Dr. Jacob R. Marcus, author and Director,
The American Jewish Archives

"We are most grateful for these materials, the importance of which is without any doubt to me. May I congratulate you on the doing of an important piece of work."
>Dr. S. Krakowski, author and Director, Yad Vashem, Jerusalem

Organizations

"Perfect for our educational/action program here. Terrific job!"
>Jeffrey Maas, Regional Director
>Anti-Defamation League, New Jersey

"...a fine publication!"
>Edward N. Leavy, Regional Director
>Anti-Defamation League, Washington, D.C.-Maryland

"...excellent: concise, clear summation"
>Morton Yarmon, National Vice President,
>American Jewish Committee

"Get this through all the Lodges!"
>South Mountain Lodge, **Bulletin,** South Orange, N.J.
>(Largest B'nai B'rith Lodge in the United States)

"...an admirable piece of work...a job well done."
>Henry W. Meyers, Chairman
>Anti-Defamation League, Asheville, N.C.

"...extremely concise, all inclusive and very helpful. The chairman of our local Holocaust Commemoration Committee, who is also a college professor of contemporary history, was very impressed by it."
>Jewish Community Center, Wilkes-Barre, Pa.

Synagogues

"Your booklet is intriguing, informative...It is about time a booklet of this type is made available."
>Rabbi Barry Dov Schwartz, Temple B'nai Sholom,
>Rockville Centre, N.Y.
>(Dr. Schwartz is an authority on Nazi war criminals in America)

"...interesting, most informative..."
>Dr. Hayyim Kieval, Chief Rabbi
>Temple Israel, Albany, N.Y.

INDEX

A

Albany Conference, 1984 ...... 60, 100
Allen, Charles R. Jr. 1, 3, 6
    10, 23, 25-28, 29, 33-34
    35-39, 46-47, 58-62, 75-77
American Nazi Party (variants of) 84-85
Anderson, Jack 16
Anti-Defamation League (ADL)..... 33
    54-55
Arrow/Cross 2, 26, 34, 43-44
Artishenko, Basil 8, 24
Artukovic, Andrija ..... ii, 6, 7, 11, 69
Assembly of Captive European
Nations (ACEN) 78-79
Aufbau.......................... 1
Auslandsorganisation (AO)
and U.S.A. 71
Avdzej, John 19

B

Barbie, Klaus ..... ii, 33, 34, 35-39, 48
Benkauskas, Henrikas 11-12, 32
Bernotas, Antanas 12
Blumenthal, Ralph............. iii, 41
    50-51, 72-74, 95
Bogdanovs, Boleslavs..... 11-12, 32,69
Bryzgys, Vincentas, Bishop 25
Buchanan, Pat 85

C

Caks, Raimunds 25
Carroll, Mons. Walter 46-47
Cases "No Longer Active,"
Listing of 19-24, 67
Cases, Summaries, Listing of..... 5, 68
Cenkus, Stasys................... 25
Central Intelligence
Agency (CIA) 6, 14, 16, 19
    22, 27, 34, 37-39
    41, 42, 56, 79-83, 84
Clements, William................ 95
Cline, Ray S. 16, 53-55
Counter Intelligence
Corps (CIC) 34, 35-39
    41-45, 52, 72-75
CROWCASS (Central Registry
of War Criminals
and Security Suspects).............35

D

D'Amato, Sen. Alfonse 16, 75-79
Dancis, Augustus................. 25
Daugavas Vanagi................. 24
Demjanjuk, John ("Ivan") 12
Denaturalization Cases,
Listing of 8-10, 64-65
Deportation Cases,
Listings of 11-18, 66
Deportation, Question of 58-69
Dercacz, Michael................. 20
Dervlag (The Flag) 33
Detlavs, Karlis................... 20
Deutscher, Albert 20
Die Spinne (The Spider)........... 37
Dora-Nordhausen (*Mittlewerke*),
Slave Labor Complex 49-56
Dornberger, Gen. Walter 56
Dougherty, Frank 18, 95
Dragonovic, Padre Stefan . 38-39, 42-48

E

Ehricke, Dr. Krafft A.F. 55-59
Eichmann, Adolf.............. 2, 48
Eilberg, Joshua 3
Ernstons, Janis Arnold 25
Extradition Requests,
by Israel........... 12, 22-23, 31, 32

F

Farago, Ladislas............... 80-82
Federal Bureau of
Investigation (FBI) 6, 25-28, 29
    32, 71-72
Fedorenko, Feodor 7, 12-13, 24
Fish, Rep. Hamilton 4
Foxman, Abraham 55
Fried, Dr. John H.E. ..., ... 60
Friedman, Milton 3
Fusion, (LaRouche
front magazine) 56
Futala, Lew..................... 25

G

Gehlen, Gen. Reinhard 53-54
Gehlen Org. 53-54
General Accounting Office (GAO)...85
Gerulaitis, Vitas.................. 25
Graham, Father Robert......... 46-47
Gudauskas, Vytautus 8, 32

H

Harel, Issar 82-83
Hazners, Vilis................. 2, 13
Hausner, Gideon 48
Helms, U.S. Sen. Jesse 84
Hilger, Gustav ii
Hier, Rabbi Marvin 74-75, 77-78
Hoenlein, Malcolm 78
Holtzman, Elizabeth 3, 55, 60-61
Hrusitzky, Anatoly 8, 20
Hudal, Bishop Alois 48
Hutyrczyk, Sergis.............. 6, 26

I

Illing, Alexander R. 26
Immigration and Naturalization
Service (INS)..........1, 19, 25-27, 30
Impulevicius, Antanas 11, 32
Iron Guard (Green Shirts)....... 2, 19
                                22, 23, 34
Iron Wolf 2, 25, 32
Israel 31

J

Jaffe, Herb......................95
Jewish War Veterans
of the U.S.A. 99
Juodis, Jurgis................. 8, 32

K

KKK (Ku Klux Klan)....... 56, 84-85
Kairys, Liudas 26
Kaminskas, Bronius 1, 6, 13
Kapos 30
Karklins, Talivaldis 20
Katin, Matthew 8, 69
Katkins, Zigurds 26
Kenyon, Richard 92
Kisielaitis, Juozas 14, 32
Klarsfeld, Beate 36
Klarsfeld, Serge 36
*Klaus Barbie and the
U.S. Government* (1983) 38-39
Klimavicius, Jonas 11-12, 32
Koppel, Ted.................. 53-54
Koreh, Ferenc 26
Kowalchuk, Mykola 9, 20
Kowalchuk, Sergei 9
Koziy, Bohdan................ 13-14
Kulle, Reinhold 14
Kungys, Juozas 9

L

LaRouche, Lyndon 56
LaVista Report, 1947 .... iii, 41-48
LaVista, Vincent 41-47
Laipenieks, Edgars......ii, 6, 14-15, 26
Lehmann, Alexander..............15
Lehman, Rep. William 4
Liberty Lobby 56, 84-85
Linnas, Karl.......... 15-16, 26, 77-79
Lipschis, Hans J. 21
Listings, Charged Nazi War
Criminals in U.S. 8-4
Littman, Sol.................. 75-77
Lithuanian Police 2nd Battalion
(*Schutzmannschaft*) 32
London Agreement, 1945 60
Lyons, Judge Francis J. 17

M

Mackevicius, Mecisiovas 26
Macs, Edmund Gustav 26
Maikovskis, Boleslavs 16-17
Manning, Cardinal Timothy 11
Martin, John 37-39
Mayer, Dr. Jean 29
Meanor, Judge H. Curtis............9
Meldon, Dr. Jerry.................29
Mendelsohn, Martin 4, 82
Mengele, Dr. Josef .... ii, 70-85
Morain, Dan 92, 95
Moulin, Jean 36
Moscow Declaration, 1943 59-60

N

National Aeronautics &
Space Agency (NASA) 50-56
Nesaule, Peter 26
Nicodemus, Charles...............95
"Nightline," ABC-TV 53-54

O

Oberlander, Theodor..............55
Office of Special Investigation
(OSI) 1, 19, 25-28, 30, 34
Office of Special Services (OSS) . 1, 19
O'Jornal................. 24, 52, 63
Organization of Ukrainian
Nationalists (OUN) 13-14, 21, 23
Osidach, Wolodymir 21, 26

P

Palciauskas, Kazys 9-10, 17, 26
Paskevicius, Mecis 17, 32
Pavelic, Ante 48
Pearson, Drew 3
Perlmutter, Nathan 16, 54-55, 78
Pius XII, Pope .... iii, 45
Popczuk, Michael 21
Popov, Ivan 27
Project Paperclip (Overcast) 49-56
Prosecution, Predicted
(by Allen) 49-56

Q

R

Rabacs, Karlis 27
Radchenko, Pavel F. 27
Radio Free Europe (RFE) ... 6, 26, 27
Radio Liberty 6
"Rat Line(s)" 38-39
Rauff, Walter 48
Rickhey, Dr. Georg .... ii, 55-56
Rockler, Walter 4
Rockwell Int'l Corp 56
Rodino, Rep. Peter W., Jr. 61-63
Roschmann, Eduard 48
Rosenbaum, Eli M. 23, 50, 62-63
Rubel, Dr. Edward 78
Ryan, Allan A., Jr. 1, 4, 7, 22
38-39, 41
Rudolph, Dr. Arthur L.H. ii
21-22, 49-55

S

"Safe Haven," Operation 41-42
Saidel, Rochelle G. 58
Samarin, Vladimir Denisovich .. 10, 27
Sautins, Karlis 27
Schatoff, M.B. 27
Schellong, Conrad 17-18
Schuk, Mykola 10
Schumer, Rep. Charles 31
Sher, Neal M. 13, 16, 24
34, 50, 69, 82
Shultz, George P.,
Sec. of State 69, 78-79
Skorzeny, Otto 37
Sokolov, Vladimir (Samarin) ... 10, 27
Soobzokov, Tscherim 22, 27
Special Litigation Unit (SLU) 4
Sprogis, Elmars 10
Stangl, Franz 48

State Department, U.S. 6, 28
34-39, 62-63, 69
Statistics, Nazi War Criminals' ... 64-69
Sterns, Alfreds 27
Strughold, Dr. Hubertus .... ii, 27
Sultanik, Kalman 62
Szalasi, Ferenc 43-44
Szulc, Johanna 24

T

Tang, Judge Thomas 15
Taylor, Myron C. 46-47
Theodorovich, George 18
Thunder Cross (*Perkonkrust*) 2, 25
Trifa, Archbishop
Valerian .... ii, 22-24, 62-63
Trucis, Arnolds 24, 28
Tufts University 29
Tulis, Peteris 28

U

U.N. War Crimes
Commission (UNWCC) 35
Ustashi 2, 34, 48

V

Vajta, Ferenc, ("Vajhta") 43-46
Vatican 35-39, 41-48
Verbelen, Robert Jan (Jean) .. 33-34, 35
Virkutis, Antanas 10
Voice of America 6
von Bolschwing,
Otto Albrecht Alfred 19
von Braun, Dr. Wernher Frhr. 49, 55-57

W

Walus, Frank (Franciszek) 24
Wanko, Annemarie 28
Warvariv, Constantine 28
Wiesenthal, Simon
(and Center) 72-78, 81-83
Williams, Judge John C. 15
Winchell, Walter 3, 45
Woerner, Ottocar Anton 28
World Anti-Communist
League (WA-CL) 55

X

Y

Yale University 10

Z

Zackevicius, Stasys 28
Zamuels, Voldemars 28
Zeltins, Teodors 28

Three Basic Books On Nazi War Criminals in the U.S.A.

Once Again...
from "America's preeminent authority..."

- **Vol. I — *From Hitler to Uncle Sam: How American Intelligence Used Nazi War Criminals — A Documentation and Commentary***

Highgate House	Illus., Appendices, Index
Fall 1985	U.S., German Intelligence Docs.
	360 pp.
	Pre-Pub. Price .... $ 9.95
	Postage & Handling (p & h) 2.50
	Total $12.45

Original... Documented... Provocative... Authoritative

- ***The Outraged Conscience Seekers of Justice for Nazi War Criminals in America***

by Rochelle G. Saidel • Preface by Beate Klarsfeld

State University of	Illus., Biblio., Index
New York Press	246 pp
1984	Paperback............. $9.95

"For this book I have waited for a long time."
Simon Wiesenthal

"A persistent cry against injustice!"
Beate Klarsfeld

"The wonderful deeds of dedicated... impressive individuals."
Prof. Ephraim Katzir,
Past President of the State of Israel

The Definitive Work

Charles R. Allen, Jr.'s

- **Vol. II — *A Nation Indicted: America's Nazi War Criminals***
  A History, Documentation and Theoretical Analysis

Highgate House	Illus., Appendices, Index
1986	1,000 pp.
Inquiries Invited	Declassified U.S. Docs.
(Trade and Public)	German Intelligence Docs.

• Charles R. Allen, Jr. has consciously related his more than 30 years of journalism to the question of fascism: its roots and causes, rallying opposition to it, seeking its eradication.

Most of his more than 1,000 by-lined articles for publications the world over, his ten books and contributions to 16 anthologies in more than a dozen languages clearly reflect this concern.

The diversity found in such works as *Concentration Camps, USA, A Measure of Freedom, Heusinger of the Fourth Reich: The Step-by-Step Resurgence of the German General Staff, The Hitler Boom and Fascism* and of course *Nazi War Criminals Among Us* nonetheless expresses a commitment to expose fascism, racism, anti-Semitism and anti-democratic repression — with primary emphasis on clarifying their social and economic essence.

Moreover, there is a distinctive stamp to this body of work; he has constantly managed to wed painstaking scholarship to his long-established record as a working investigative reporter. (Said *The Saturday Evening Post* — even while trying in the 1960's to debunk his *Concentration Camps, USA* — "...he documents the document." Said *The Washington Star* in the late 1970's about his personally tracking down over 150 Nazi war criminals living in the United States who had been used by various agencies of the government: "He's very careful and tough. Very.")

These dynamic forces come together in *A Nation Indicted: America's Nazi War Criminals* which examines this profoundly ominous phenomenon within the implications found in the familiar question: Can It Happen Here?

Indeed, *A Nation Indicted* contends that a Nazi war criminal presence in — and, most importantly, its utilization by — post-Holocaust America can only have meaning when considered precisely within such a context:

• What relationships obtain between American monopoly corporations, banks, ranking research institutions and utilization of proven fascist criminals? • Was there a monopoly presence in the huge operation called Project Paperclip that brought to our shores 1,558 German and Austrian scientists — most of who were Nazi Party members, some SS officers, and more than a few participants in crimes against humanity? • Is there a symbiosis among SS murder squads on the Russian Front, the origins of American counter-insurgency in the 1950's and the 1984 CIA booklet instructing U.S.-backed counter-revolutionaries to kidnap, torture and assassinate in order to overthrow the government of Nicaragua? The questions — basic, endemic to the American system — multiply.

The answers — always complex, difficult, often tentative — suggest where America — *A Nation Indicted* — may well be headed.

Acknowledgements: I wish to thank the following publications, editors and news services for their kind permission to cite and use selections from my own writings and reportage that they first published: *The Boston Globe,* Alan Berger, Tom Gaigan; *The Los Angeles Times; The Miami News,* John Hopkins; *Newsday,* Toby Frankel; *The New York Times; The Times-Union,* Harry Rosenfeld and the Hearst Newspapers syndicate. The Jewish Telegraphic Agency (JTA), Murray Zuckoff; Associated Press (AP). *The Churchman,* Edna Ruth Johnson; *Israel Horizons,* Aviva Cantor; *Jewish Currents,* Morris U. Schappes; *The Jewish Veteran,* Joan Alpert, Bob Stone; *Martyrdom & Resistance,* Eli Zborowski, Harvey Rosenfeld; *Morgan Freiheit,* Chaim Suller; *The New Statesman; Reform Judaism* and *Keeping Posted,* Aron Hirt-Manheimer, Steven Schnur. Also my thanks to the following TV programs for permission to cite transcripts of their shows with which I was associated and appeared on: "Close-Up," ABC News, Pamela Hill, Richard Girdaux, Michael Connor; ABC's "Good Morning, America," Hugh Downes, David Hartman; "Nightline," ABC News, Ted Koppel, Steve Lewis, Heather Vincent, Sergio Guerrero; ABC News, John Martin; CBS Morning News, Dianne Sawyer. On radio, my thanks as always to Studs Terkel and Al Angeloro, NBC Radio. My appreciation and abiding respect also go to an especially select band on this beat: Ralph Blumenthal of *The New York Times,* Frank Dougherty of *The Philadelphia Daily News,* Herb Jaffe, *The Star-Ledger* of Newark, N.J., Richard Kenyon of *The Milwaukee Journal,* Dan Morain of *The Los Angeles Times,* and Charlie Nicodemus and the late Bill Clemens of the dearly missed *Chicago Daily News* and *The Chicago Sun Times.*

Please Tear Out
Along Edge for Mailing Orders

ORDER FORM

Please send your order with check or money order to:

**Highgate House
P.O. Box 986
Fort George Station
New York, NY 10040-9998**

Enclosed is $ _____ for items indicated below
(including postage & handling). ***Do not send cash!***

Please send _____ copies of:

Nazi War Criminals in America: Facts... Action
The Basic Handbook

@ $6.95 per single copy
+ $2.50 for postage & handling for each copy

$5.50 each for 2 to 9 copies + p & h ($2.00 ea. copy)

$5.00 each for 10 or more sent to same address
+ p & h ($2.00 ea. copy)

Larger bulk rates available upon request.
(Above applies to both U.S. and Canada)

Name _____

Street Address _____

City _____ State _____ Zip _____

ORDER FORM

Yes, I wish to receive the following books:

Title —	Number of Copies	Price + P & H
● *From Hitler to Uncle Sam: How American Intelligence Used Nazi War Criminals* by Charles R. Allen, Jr.	_____	**$9.95** ea. + **$2.50** (Pre-Pub. only) **Total ea. = $12.45**
● *The Outraged Conscience Seekers of Justice for Nazi War Criminals in America* by Rochelle G. Saidel	_____	**$9.95** ea. + **$2.50** **Total ea. = $12.45**

Name _____

Street Address _____

City _____ State _____ Zip _____

Enclosed is $_____ for items checked above,
(including postage & handling)

(Note: *A Nation Indicted: America's Nazi War Criminals* will not be available until 1986.
Inquiries — from the Trade and Public — about the book are welcome.)

Please send your order with check or money order to:
Highgate House
P.O. Box 986
Fort George Station
New York, NY 10040-9998